A Basic Guide To
DECATHLON

An Official U.S. Olympic Committee Sports Series

The U.S. Olympic Committee

Griffin Publishing

10 9 8 7 6 5 4 3 2 1

ISBN 1 882180 68 2

Griffin Publishing

544 W. Colorado Street
Glendale, California 91204

Telephone: 1-818-244-2128 / Fax 1-818-242-1172

Manufactured in the United States of America

Acknowledgments

PUBLISHER

Robert M. Howland
President, Griffin Publishing

U.S.O.C.

United States Olympic Committee
One Olympic Plaza
Colorado Springs, CO 80909-5760
John Krimsky, Jr.,
Deputy Secretary General

Barry King
Mike Moran
Bob Paul

SERIES EDITOR

Richard D. Burns, Ph.D.

WRITER

Frank Zarnowski, Ph.D.

EDITOR

Freda Yoshioka

BOOK DESIGN

Mark M. Dodge

COORDINATOR

Robin L. Howland

CONTRIBUTOR

Barry King

The United States Olympic Committee

The United States Olympic Committee is the custodian of the U.S. Olympic Movement and is dedicated to providing opportunities for American athletes of all ages. The U.S. Olympic Committee, a streamlines organization of member organizations, is the moving force for the support of sports in the United States that are on the program of the Olympic and/or Pan American Games, or those wishing be included.

The USOC is recognized by the International Olympic Committee as the sole agency in the United States whose mission involves training, entering, and underwriting the full expenses for the United States teams in the Olympic and Pan American Games.

The USOC also supports the bid of U.S. cities to host the winter and summer Olympic Games, or the winter and summer Pan American Games and, after reviewing all the candidates, votes on and may endorse one city per event as the U.S. bid city. The USOC also selects the cities which will host its own U.S. Olympic Festival and approve U.S. trial sites for the Olympic and Pan American Games team selections.

Welcome to the Olympic Sports Series

We are extremely pleased to inaugurate the Olympic Sports Series. I feel this unique series will encourage parents, athletes of all ages and novices who are thinking about a sport for the first time, to get involved with the challenging and rewarding world of Olympic sports.

This series of paperback books covers both summer and winter sports, features Olympic history and basic sports fundamentals, and encourages family involvement. Each book includes information on how to get started in a particular sport, including equipment and clothing; rules of the game; health and fitness; basic first aid; and guidelines for spectators. Of special interest is the information on opportunities for senior citizens, volunteers and physically challenged athletes. In addition, each book is enhanced by photographs and illustrations and a complete, easy-to-understand glossary.

Because this family-oriented series neither assumes nor requires prior knowledge of a particular sport, it can be enjoyed by all age groups. Regardless of anyone's level of sports knowledge, playing experience or athletic ability, this official U.S. Olympic Committee Sports Series will encourage understanding and participation in sports and fitness.

The purchase of these books will assist the 1996 U.S. Olympic Team. This series supports the Olympic mission and serves importantly to enhance participation in the Olympic and Pan American Games.

John Krimsky, Jr.

Deputy Secretary General

About the Author...

Frank Zarnowski, Ph.D., is a professor of economics at Mt. St. Mary's College, Emmitsburg, Maryland. Dr. Zarnowski has authored numerous books on the subject of the decathlon and has served as television commentator and public address announcer for decathlon competitions. He has been a longtime fan of the sport.

Contents

USA

An Athelete's Creed

The most important thing in the Olympic Games is not to win but to take part, just as the most important thing in life is not the triumph but the struggle. The essential thing is not to have conquered but to have fought well.

These famous words, commonly referred to as the Olympic Creed, were once spoken by Baron Pierre de Coubertin, founder of the modern Olympic Games. Whatever their origins, they aptly describe the theme behind each and every Olympic competition.

THE DECATHLON IN OLYMPIC HISTORY

THE JIM THORPE STORY

When King Gustav V of Sweden presented awards at the 1912 Olympic Games of Stockholm, he declared to the decathlon winner, an American Indian named Jim Thorpe: "You, sir, are the world's greatest athlete." Jim is purported to have replied, "Thanks, King." This story, true or not, has become part of the Thorpe saga.

Ever since, the Olympic decathlon champion or world recordholder has been dubbed the "World's Greatest Athlete." This is an appropriate title since the decathlon is the only objective test of all-around athletic ability. Decathletes must contest 10 separate events and have those performances tallied against a standard scoring table. The decathlon measures basic sporting abilities like jumping, sprinting and throwing. Within the context of the rules of track and field, decathlon champions must exhibit the four S's: Speed, Spring, Strength and Stamina.

Since 1912, great decathlon champions such as Bob Mathias, Rafer Johnson, Bruce Jenner, and Daley

Thompson have become household names. All of these athletes owe much to the legend of Thorpe.

In 1912 Jim Thorpe, a Native American from the Sac and Fox tribe, was a student at the Carlisle (Pa.) Indian School and was already being called "the athletic marvel of the age." As one of the nation's top football players, he turned his attention to the Stockholm Olympic Games. Thorpe made the U.S. team in four events and won gold medals in the first Olympic decathlon and pentathlon.

Photo courtesy of the Cumberland County Historical Society

Jim Thorpe, winner of the first Olympic decathlon crown in 1912.

A year later, Thorpe was stripped of his Olympic records and medals when it was discovered that he had played professional baseball for a few dollars—not unusual for students of the day. Nonetheless, the Amateur Athletic Union (AAU) of the United States made an example of Thorpe, claiming he was not a true amateur. It was a raw deal and Thorpe left

Carlisle and became a professional athlete. He played major and minor league baseball for 10 more seasons and professional football until 1929, when he was 41. He was even the National Football League's (NFL) first president. No one surpassed his decathlon score for 15 years. In 1953 Jim Thorpe was voted the "Athlete of the First Half Century."

In 1982, 29 years after Jim Thorpe's penniless death, the International Olympic Committee (IOC) restored his name to the Olympic record books and presented his children with facsimile medals in January 1983.

Jim's Native American heritage, remarkable athletic ability, and long professional careers make him one of the most prominent figures in American sports history. The loss of his Olympic medals elevated him to an almost martyr-like status. Even today, eight decades later, of all decathlon men, his name is still history's most recognizable.

THE ANCIENT PENTATHLON

In one sense, modern decathlon history begins with the Thorpe story. In a larger sense, the story begins 26 centuries earlier. The Ancient Greeks created an all-around test, the pentathlon, for their Olympic Games. The ancient pentathlon consisted of a long jump, discus throw, javelin throw, a sprint and ended with a wrestling match. There is still considerable academic debate regarding the order of events and how the winner was determined.

To ascertain their best all-around athletes, the Ancient Greeks found that five (*penta*) events were satisfactory, compared to the 10 (*deca*) used by modern Olympians. The pentathlon emphasized speed andstrength. Technique and endurance played lesser roles.

Source: F.A.M. Webster's The Evolution of the Olympic Games, 1829 B.C.–1914 A.D.

An Ancient Greek amphora depicts several of the pentathlon events: discus, long jump, and javelin.

Much like the first day of the modern decathlon, the ancient pentathlon was power oriented. According to most evidence, wrestling was the last event and necessary only if the pentathlon winner had not been determined in the earlier events.

The pentathlon was introduced in Olympia in 708 B.C. and continued uninterrupted every fourth year for almost 11 centuries. The first Olympic pentathlon winner was Lampis, a young Spartan. Although the Ancient Greeks did not keep records as we do today (there is no way to say "break a record" or "set a record" in Ancient Greek language), we do have the names of many of the pentathlon winners.

The pentathlon was not just an Olympic event. By the sixth century B.C. major religious games were held in Corinth, Delphi and Nemea. Secondary athletic festivals were conducted in most towns. Athletes could and did compete in numerous pentathlons annually.

The popularity of the pentathlon varied over time and from person to person. Some, like Aristotle, had lofty respect for the pentathlete's combination of speed and strength. Others, like wrestler Plato (his name means "broad shouldered"), considered the pentathlete a mediocre performer. In contrast, the poet Bacchlylides, in an ode to the winner, leaves little doubt about his sentiment for Automedes, winner of a Nemean Games pentathlon:

He shone among the other pentathletes as the bright moon in the middle of the month dims the radiance of the stars: even thus he showed his lovely body to the great ring of watching Greeks, as he threw the round discus and hurled the shaft of black leaved elder (javelin) from his grasp to the steep heights of heaven, and roused the cheers of the spectators by his lithe movements in the wrestling at the end.

Olympians, including the pentathletes, were hardly amateurs in modern terms; they were paid for their efforts. By the 5th Century B.C., city states bid for the services of athletes and generously rewarded them for major victories. Today's most authoritative scholar of Ancient Olympics, David C. Young, estimates that a pentathlon victory, which could be paid in a variety of forms (for example, jars of olive oil), was worth more money than a full year's labor.

The last recorded ancient Olympic pentathlon winner was Publius Asklepiades of Corinth who won in A.D. 241. In A.D. 393 Roman Emperor Theodosius I, a Christian, closed all non-Christian sanctuaries, including Olympia, effectively ending the ancient Olympic Games. The site was abandoned and over the centuries, buried by nature and earthquakes. It would be more than 15 centuries before another Olympic multi-event winner would be crowned. In the 19th century German archaeological teams excavated the ancient Olympic site. Soon thereafter the Greek organizers and the French Baron Pierre de Coubertin promoted a revival of the Olympic Games.

THE MIDDLE AGES

The importance of athletics (and therefore multi-event competitions) deteriorated as Greek and Roman civilization declined. However, the ideal of a versatile, all-around athlete never disappeared during the 15 centuries that the world went without Olympic Games.

During the Viking era (approximately A.D. 800-1250) Norsemen had to pass a number of athletic tests, military in nature. Multi-event contests for Vikings included running, wrestling, throwing heavy spears and even dashing over moving oars. Medieval knights periodically tested their skills in tournaments, many of which used a point scoring system. Aspirants had to pass multi-event tests before knighthood.

Treatises on educational reform in the middle of the 16th century called for youths to know how to ride in armor, vault on horseback, practice weightlifting, run, wrestle and jump for distance and height.

By the early 17th century Robert Dover, an aristocratic English lawyer, reinstated the Olympic Games. These annual affairs, the Olympik Games of the Cotswolds, began in 1612 and lasted more than two centuries. Thousands, including William Shakespeare, came to watch the Cotswold Olympik Games.

Unfortunately, the Dover Olympiks contained no multi-event contest. Nonetheless, the values of the the period were conducive to the development of multi-event contests. The Renaissance stressed versatility and the Enlightenment, which developed new ideas about physical education, would provide the setting for future multi-event contests. Advancements in technology and economics provided Europeans with free time to pursue physical fitness for its own sake.

In the mid-1700s in Dessau (today's Germany), students competed in a school pentathlon. Although based on the Ancient Greek version, this pentathlon also tested knighthood skills. A little later, in 1792 in Stockholm, Swedes crowned an overall champion of a three-event contest that included running, throwing a large stone, and swimming.

In the late 18th century, Guts Muth, the German author of the first book on physical education, developed a forerunner of modern decathlon scoring tables. On a weekly basis, he awarded points for his pupils' running, jumping and swimming performances. Guts Muth and later 19th century German reformers anticipated much of today's decathlon.

Meanwhile, track and field staged a comeback in the first half of the 19th century and it would not be long before multi-events joined the movement. Modern track expert and historian Roberto Quercetani claims that all-around competitions were held in Ireland in the middle of the 19th century. Another English Olympic revival, the Much Wenlock Games, offered a pentathlon in 1851 that included a high jump, a long jump, putting a 36-pound stone, a half-mile run and climbing a 55-foot rope.

Large numbers of Scots, Irish and Germans emigrated to America during the 19th century and they brought their games with them. The Scottish Caledonian Games, German Turners and U.S. colleges fostered the return of track and field, which became popular after the Civil War. Many American meets had an "all-around winner," usually the athlete winning the most events or places. The concept was formalized in 1884 when the AAU designed a national All-Around Championship. This evolved into a grueling 10-event contest (100-yard run, shot put, high jump, 880-yard walk, hammer throw, pole vault, 120-yard hurdles, 56-pound weight throw, long jump and 1-mile run) performed in a single day, with only 5 minutes rest between events. Winners had to meet minimum marks in each event and were scored on a points-for-place basis until 1893 when the newly formed AAU generated a scoring table to evaluate each performance.

In 1880 the German Gymnastics Championship featured and all-around championship. It included a stone throw, pole vault and long jump. By the 1890s several Scandinavian nations were offering a pentathlon, exactly the same as the ancient Greek event. When the Olympic Games were renewed in 1896 in Athens, Greece, a multi-event contest was overlooked, as it would be in Paris 4 years later. However, in 1904, the AAU held its All-Around Championship in conjunction with the Olympic Games of St. Louis. Irishman Tom Kiely won easily, becoming the first Olympic multi-event track champion in 16 centuries.

In 1906, 10-year anniversary Olympic Games were held in Athens and organizers, searching for a multi-event contest, conducted the ancient Greek pentathlon, complete with wrestling. Two years later the British, as they have for most of the 20th century, neglected multi-events at the 1908 London Olympic Games. It was up to the Swedes to include multi-event contests at the 1912 Olympic Games of Stockholm and they did so with gusto. The Swedish organizers planned a "modern" pentathlon based on military events, a track and field pentathlon based on the ancient variety (substituting the 1500-meter run for wrestling) and a decathlon, a 10-event contest.

The word *decathlon* (*deka*, "ten;" *athlos*, "contest") was first used in Scandinavia (Danish *tikamp*) and (Swedish *tiokamp*). Both Denmark and Sweden offered "decathlons" in the early years of the 20th century with different events, order and tables. In 1911, using today's 10 events and sequence, the Swedes conducted the first modern decathlon as a rehearsal for the Stockholm Olympic Games a year later. The decathlon has not changed since. The Göteborg winner was Hugo Weislander who would finish second to Jim Thorpe and would later inherit the world record and Thorpe's medal.

MODERN DECATHLON HISTORY

The Scandinavians displayed an immediate affinity for the decathlon. All but one of the Olympic decathletes who received medals before World War II were from either the United States or a Scandinavian nation. American achievements were chiefly the result of talented ex-collegians from America's heartland taking up the event once every 4 years. Scandinavian success was evidence of a multifaceted view of physical education.

The Berlin Olympic Games, scheduled for 1916, were canceled because of World War I. In 1920 Norwegian soldier Helge Lövland edged Brutus Hamilton of the University of Missouri by the smallest margin, before or since, in Olympic decathlon history. Hamilton, while coaching at the University of California at Berkely, became one of America's best-loved and most successful mentors. Four years later, in 113-degree heat on Paris' 500-meter track, Harold Osborn, a former student at the University of Illinois, won the gold medal just days after he also won the Olympic high-jump title. He remains the only athlete to have won both the decathlon and an individual event.

In 1928 in Amsterdam, a pair of Finns, Paavo Yröjla and Akilles Järvinen, captured the gold and silver medals. Steady Ken Doherty of Detroit, Michigan won the bronze. Doherty's track career spanned six decades. Like Hamilton, he became one of America's best-known coaches (Universities of Michigan and Pennsylvania). Doherty was also the director of the prestigious Penn Relays and author of popular track and field textbooks books.

A Kansas University football and basketball star, "Jarring" Jim Bausch turned back Järvinen at the Los Angeles Olympic Games in 1932. Bausch is still regarded as the greatest athlete in the history of Kansas University. This is quite an accomplishment since four-time Olympic discus winner Al Oerter, Olympic 10k champ Billy Mills and hoop star Wilt Chamberlain were all Jayhawks, too. Ironically, had later sets of scoring tables been used in both 1928 and 1932, Järvinen would have had higher totals than either winner. Such is the subjectivity of the scoring tables.

Germans expected their world-record holder, Hans-Heinrich Sievert, to win the Olympic gold medal in Berlin in 1936. The United States came up with a used-car salesman from Denver named Glenn Morris, a former football star at Colorado State. Morris took up the decathlon in 1936 and broke Sievert's record in just his second meet. However, the great Morris-Sievert duel never took place because the German came down with a mysterious illness. Morris broke his own world record and led a first, second and third-place U.S. sweep (all brilliantly captured by Leni Riefenstahl's superb film, *Olympiad, Festival of Nations.*). Morris immediately retired, undefeated in the decathlon, but made nothing of a Hollywood career, appearing with the lead role in but one film, *Tarzan's Revenge.*

World War II robbed several all-around greats of Olympic opportunities. The most notable was Michigan's Big Bill Watson who would have been the decathlon favorite both in 1940 and 1944.

THE POST WAR ERA

In 1948 at the London Olympic Games, a 17-year old schoolboy from California turned all the decathlon traditions upside down. Until then, most Olympic decathletes had been older and more experienced athletes. Yet here was Mathias, during two miserable days of London fog, turning back the world's best. And it was only his third decathlon. He was, and still is, the youngest track and field champion in Olympic history.

In the intervening years, Mathias enrolled at Stanford, starred as a running back and broke and rebroke the decathlon world record. At the 1952 Helsinki Games, Mathias became the first decathlete to win a pair of Olympic titles. He led another U.S. sweep and won by more than 900 points, the largest margin in Olympic history. Although just 21, Bob retired, undefeated and four-time national champion. He starred in the movie version of his life, *The Bob Mathias Story*, then served several terms in Congress and was director of the

United States Olympic Training Center in Colorado Springs.

The Helsinki Games saw an American sweep of all decathlon medals. New Jersey schoolboy Milt Campbell garnered the silver and Floyd Simmons captured his second bronze. Four years later Campbell conquered American teammate and world-record holder Rafer Johnson at the 1956 Melbourne Olympic Games. Milt was one of the most versatile athletes of any age. One year later he broke the world record for the 120-yard hurdles, then turn to a professional football career. He was also a national class judo competitor and All-American swimmer. He is the only athlete inducted into both the National Swimming and National Track and Field Halls of Fame.

Much like Milt Campbell 4 years earlier, Rafer Johnson stepped up from silver to gold, winning the decathlon at the 1960 Olympic Games in Rome, Italy. It was not easy. He had to contend with UCLA teammate, C.K. Yang of Formosa (now Taiwan). For two hot Italian days and nights they put a moratorium on their friendship and battled for 10 events at Rome's Estadio Olympico. With only the 1500 meters remaining, Johnson led by 67 points. If Yang could put 10 seconds between himself and Rafer, he would win the gold medal. Rafer dogged C.K.'s every step, finished a few meters back and won by a slim margin. Italian spectators chanted, "Give them both the gold medal, give them both the gold medal."

Photo courtesy of Hershey's Track and Field Youth Program

Rafer Johnson won the most dramatic Olympic decathlon, defeatingC.K. Yang in Rome in 1960.

A NEW DECATHLON ERA

The 1960s saw the decathlon come of age. American Phil Mulkey and C.K. Yang took turns breaking Rafer

Johnson's world record. Then, in 1964, the International Amateur Athletic Federation (IAAF) introduced new scoring tables, making the decathlon a more balanced event. No longer could a handful of good events win the decathlon. However, a decathlete could now lose with just one bad event. Decathletes now had to be proficient in *every* event. West German coach Friedel Schirmer, who finished eighth at the 1952 Helsinki decathlon, raised his nation's awareness and popularity of the decathlon. Schirmer insisted that the decathlon was not 10 unrelated events, but an event in itself. Balance and focus on the new tables were the hallmarks of his training methods. As a result, his athletes were very successful during the decade. In 1964 in Tokyo, the American decathlon winning streak, which began in 1932, ended. Germans Willy Holdorf and Hans-Joachim Walde won the gold and bronze, sandwiching Estonian Rein Aun. Paul Herman from little Westmont College (Calif.), was fourth and all topped Yang.

Four years later Schirmer's athletes claimed *all* the Olympic medals. American Bill Toomey, a Santa Barbara English teacher, had trained with Schirmer in West Germany for 1 year. Toomey, Walde and his world-record holder teammate Kurt Bendlin won first second and third places at the Mexico City Games of 1968. Toomey's victory stands apart from those of earlier prominent American decathletes. He was considerably older (his 1969 world record came just before his 31st birthday) and he competed a great deal more. His numerous efforts proved that a well-trained decathlete could compete frequently at a world-class level. Bill competed in 38 career decathlons, compared to the combined total of 26 for Mathias, Campbell and Johnson.

Bill's training partner, Russ Hodge, had broken the world record in 1966 but was often injured. Toomey's career was even more remarkable since, as a youngster, he severed all the nerves in his right wrist and lost almost all sensation. He rebuilt the wrist with therapy but the hand bothered him throughout his career. In spite of the adversity, Bill won 23 major decathlon meets including five U.S. national titles (still a record) and the Olympic gold!

Eastern European nations, especially the Soviet Union, Poland and East Germany, began to emphasize and promote the decathlon in the early 1970s. At the 1972 Munich Games Toomey watched from the ABC television platform as a Soviet, the lanky Nikolay Avilov, replaced him as *both* Olympic champion and world-record holder. Another Soviet, soldier Leonid Litvenyenko, and Ryszard Katus of Poland, won the remaining medals. The top American, diminutive Jeff Bennett, lost the bronze medal to Katus (who later defected to the United States) by a mere 10 points. Bennett, who attended tiny Oklahoma Christian College, stood but 5 feet 8 inches and weighed only 152 pounds. Although slight in build, he was a fierce competitor and had the heart of a giant. His battle for the final medal in Munich was the closest in Olympic decathlon annals. An unnoticed but respectable 10th in Munich was a little known American named Bruce Jenner.

Photo courtesy of Chartmasters

Bruce Jenner set a new decathlon world record in 1976 while winning the Olympic gold medal in Montreal.

THE AGE OF BOYCOTTS

Jenner had set two world decathlon records in the months before the Olympic Games of 1976 and

Montreal was to be a showdown with the defending champion, Avilov. From the opening gun it was obvious that Jenner was on a roll and after the first day, he was just a few points behind German Guido Kratschmer and Avilov. His best events came on the second day and Jenner steamrolled the field. With only the 1500 meters remaining, the question was not whether Jenner would raise his own world record, but by how much. Unlike most decathletes, he looked forward to running the last event.

As Jenner rested on the infield, Litvenyenko tapped him on the shoulder and predicted, "Bruce, you are going to be Olympic champion." "Thanks," Bruce replied. Litvenyenko gazed at Jenner for a few moments and then asked, "Bruce, are you going to be a millionaire?" Jenner merely laughed in response. In the 1500 meters Jenner ran conservatively at first, then gunned it at the bell, clocking the final 400 meters in an eye-opening 61 seconds. He had recorded a lifetime best in his final event, 4:12.61, and a gaping world record, 8618 points. Someone shoved an American flag in his hand and he took his victory lap on prime-time television.

In Africa, the decathlon is not yet a well-developed sport. Therefore, African nations' boycott of the 1976 Olympic Games did not have much effect on the decathlon results. The burly and bearded Kratschmer won the silver medal and Avilov settled for the bronze. Jenner retired without delay, even leaving his vaulting poles in the Montreal stadium tunnel. For him there would be new worlds to conquer. Although, he did recall that one athlete who had finished 18th, a British teenager named Daley Thompson, had asked a lot of questions.

Another boycott occurred in 1980. This one was led by U.S. President Jimmy Carter. American and German track and field contingents did not participate in the Moscow Olympic Games, robbing the decathlon field of two excellent contenders. Texan Bob Coffman, the Pan American champion as well as the new world-record holder, and Guido Kratschmer, missed their chances to compete. The British team did travel to the Soviet Union and Daley Thompson was not seriously challenged. Daley began his 1980s reign, now labeled, the "Daley decade."

Thompson won the European crown in 1982 in Athens with a new world record, then captured the International Amateur Athletic Federation's (IAAF) initial World Championship in Helsinki in 1983. In both cases he vanquished giant Jürgen Hingsen, called the "German Hercules." The Thompson/ Hingsen affairs of the 1980s were classics. The pair broke and rebroke the world record on seven occasions; but, head-to-head, Thompson never lost.

In 1984, when the Olympic Games returned to the United States for the first time in 52 years, it was the Eastern bloc nations, led by the Soviets, who stayed at home. As Thompson was once again supreme, the boycott had little impact on the decathlon. Daley, like Bob Mathias before him, won a second gold medal, again broke the world record and *again* made Hingsen settle for the silver. West German Siggi Wentz won the bronze and it is difficult to envision any Eastern bloc decathletes who could have broken up the top three. Two years later at the 1986 European Championship in Stuttgart, West Germany, the

Thompson-Hingsen-Wentz trio again won first, second and third places in what many still consider to be the best international decathlon ever.

In 1987 an injury slowed Daley at the second World Championship in Rome. Then 29 years old, he competed anyway and finished ninth, his first defeat in nine seasons. Hingsen, suffering broken ribs, did not finish. In their absence, East Germany's Torsten Voss, a 24-year old mechanic, held off Wentz for the win.

At the Seoul Olympic Games of 1988, favorite Siggi Wentz was injured and could not compete. Thompson, then 30 years old and in his fourth Olympics, was injured and short on conditioning. Nevertheless, he entered the arena. There he watched a 6-foot 6-inch East German medical student, Christian Schenk, use a 7-foot 5-inch high jump to earn the gold medal. Voss was second and Canadian Dave Steen, a University of California, Berkeley, student, edged Thompson for the bronze medal.

The 1980s witnessed a terrific run by Thompson: 12 consecutive wins, all in major meets. He managed to triumph over top competition. The decade also witnessed an explosion of the number of world-class decathletes. A score of more than 8000 points, once nearly unheard of, was bettered more than 500 times in the 1980s, with the Soviets and Germans (West and East) far ahead of the rest of the world. For Americans it was the worst decade yet. In the first 8 years of the 1980s, Americans barely reached the annual world rankings.

ENTER DAN & DAVE

After the 1988 Seoul Olympic Games, American decathlon fortunes abruptly reversed course. Californian Dave Johnson led the resurgence and his score for 1989 topped the world list. In 1990 credit card company VISA, USA, Inc. initiated a national program to help restore U.S. decathlon prominence. Later that year, Johnson and Dan O'Brien, a former University of Idaho star, swept the Goodwill Games decathlon in Seattle. Again, Johnson's best score topped the world list. A year later it was O'Brien who threatened Daley Thompson's world record and who captured the third World Championship crown in Tokyo. Decathlon circles credited VISA for reviving U.S. decathlon strength.

In 1992 the athletic shoe company Reebok featured both O'Brien and Johnson in a multi-million dollar advertising campaign entitled, "Dan or Dave? To Be Settled in Barcelona." The campaign increased decathlon popularity in the Unites States but neither O'Brien nor Johnson were fortunate enough to win at the 1992 Barcelona Olympic Games. O'Brien, suffering a stress fracture, was unable to clear a pole vault bar at the U.S. Olympic Trials and did not make the U.S. team. Johnson won the Trials but suffered a broken bone in his foot just weeks before the games. He kept the injury secret, competed anyway, and limped home with the bronze medal. Czechoslovakia's Robert Zmelik won in Barcelona and Spain's Antonio Penalver was second. One month later, O'Brien met Zmelik at DecaStar, an invitational decathlon in Talence, France. Not only did the American win by more than 500 points but he broke Daley Thompson's 8-year-old world record, running up 8891 points. O'Brien's score is the current world record.

Photo courtesy of Victah Sailer

Dave Johnson

Photo courtesy of Iris Hensel

Dan O'Brien

One year later, O'Brien captured another world title, this time in Stuttgart, Germany, where his major foes were Eduard Hämäläinen of Belorussia and Germany's tall Paul Meier. In 1994 Hämäläinen had the world's top score, 8735 points, while O'Brien went undefeated with three efforts over 8700. One year later O'Brien won a third IAAF World Championship where, once again, Hämäläinen was his main rival. Hämäläinen, O'Brien plus American Steve Fritz and Commonwealth champion Michael Smith will be the major medal contenders in 1996 at the Atlanta Olympic Games.

2

THE NATURE OF THE DECATHLON

Size, Events & Rules

The decathlon is a 2-day miniature track meet designed to ascertain the sport's best all-around athlete. Participants compete in 10 different track and field (athletics) contests and are scored against an international scoring table for each event. The winner is the athlete with the highest total score.

Within the rules of track and field, each athlete must sprint for 100 meters, long jump, heave a 16-pound ball, high jump and run 400 meters, all in that very order, on the first day. On the second day the athlete runs a 110-meter hurdle race over ten 42-inch barriers, hurls the discus, pole vaults, tosses a javelin and, and the end of the contest, races 1500 meters, about a mile.

The decathlon is an Olympic multi-event sport for men. The women's counterpart is a seven-event contest called the "heptathlon." Almost all of the decathlon information applies to the women's heptathlon. The heptathlon consists of the 100-meter hurdles, high jump, long jump and 200 meters on the first day. On the second day the events are the long jump, javelin and 800 meters.

Many athletic disciplines, from gymnastics to rodeo to Nordic skiing to equestrian, have all-around contests. However, track and field represents the most fundamental sport in which athletes run, jump and throw. The decathlon measures these fundamental athletic talents in terms of speed, strength, agility, spring and endurance. While one athlete may be faster, another stronger and yet a third a better jumper, the decathlon attempts to determine who, among the three, is the best all-around or general athlete.

The skills of the decathlete are not specific to any sport. Although all sporting contests require fast, strong and agile athletes, they also demand specific skills. For example, making a 20-foot jump shot, hitting a curve ball or kicking a field goal are difficult to master and specific to certain sports. They are not general in nature. This is why decathlon champions may be the best *all-around* athletes in the world. Making a case that decathletes are the "world's best athletes" is harder. Some athletes with honed *specific* talents, for example Michael Jordan or Ken Griffey, Jr., may be so proficient in their unique skills that they overshadow a decathlete with terrific general competency.

The decathlete does not have to be exceptional in any one event to be the champion of 10 events. He must range from being at least adequate in his weak events to outstanding in his stronger events. Because the decathlete must do well in three running, one hurdling, three jumping and three throwing events, he has less opportunity to perfect and polish any one of the events. So he must compromise. This is the nature of the decathlon. The decathlete must make strategic concessions in his preparations to maximize the total score. In training he must strive to improve technique, gain strength without sacrificing speed or spring, and vice versa. At the same time, he must acquire the endurance to escort him through a competition which, in many cases, lasts 8–10 hours each day.

The decathlon is the only event in which it doesn't really matter if the athlete finishes first, third or worse in a particular event. Since the number is what matters, the decathlete competes against the scoring table. In other words, he competes against his own ability and IAAF standards.

Photo courtesy of Victah Sailer

Mental factors play an important role: Decathletes must stay focused for 2 days of competition.

A score of 8000 points (averaging 800 points per event) is a rule-of-thumb cutoff for world-class decathletes. Few major international meetings will be won with a score of less than 8000 points.

Mental factors play a great role in the decathlon. Many coaches talk of a "decathlon mentality." This refers to the athlete's ability to stay focused throughout the 10 events, to get psyched up for each attempt or race, and to shrug off disappointment and get on with the next trial. In the decathlon there are chances to recuperate from mistakes.

Decathletes also differ from many athletes in their reactions to a completed meet. Ask a decathlete to asses his recently completed performance and he is invariably dissatisfied. Rarely does a decathlete achieve personal record (PR) performance in every event. No matter how well he performs, whether he wins or sets a record, the decathlete can always find room for improvement. There is always a "wait until next time" attitude.

In the decathlon the opponent is rarely another athlete. Consequently, the decathlon is the most neighborly of all track events. The same athletes are together for most of two days and the rules require a minimum of 30-minutes rest between events. There is a lot of time to chat on the field. Much of the time is used helping one another, appraising technique, verifying takeoff points, giving advice and reassurance, and even sharing equipment.

The struggle is against time, distance, fatigue and one's inner fear of weakness or failure and the scoring tables. The opponent is oneself; other decathletes are comrades, friends who help one another do his best.

Rarely are they hostile. Each decathlete concentrates on doing his best without diminishing the efforts of others.

DECATHLETES COME IN ALL SHAPES & SIZES

Unlike wrestling or boxing, there are no weight classes in the decathlon. World-class competitors have been as small as Jeff Bennett who was 5 feet 8 inches and weighed just under 150 pounds when he first broke 8000 points back in 1970. In contrast, Rick Wanamaker was a 6-foot 8-inch, 210-pound center on the Drake University basketball team. Bennett was an Olympic competitor while Wanamaker was the first National Collegiate Athletic Association (NCAA) decathlon champion. Few have been heavier than Rudy Ziegert's 235 pounds or Russ Hodge's 225. The former, a Soviet soldier, scored more than 8000 points on numerous occasions. Hodge held the world record in 1966.

Here is a range of heights and weights for most world-class competitors:

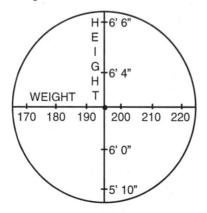

Average Size 6' 2", 195 lbs.

Just as decathletes score a wide range of points on the scoring tables, decathletes possess a wide range of shapes, sizes and body types. However, as athletes approach world-class levels, their sizes become remarkably similar. The average height is about 6 feet to 6 feet 3 inches and the weight ranges from 180–200 pounds. This *may* be an "ideal" size. Nevertheless, many successful decathletes have been small and wiry, tall and rangy, short and bulky, and tall and bulky. Many do not fit the ideal description.

Here is a range of heights and weights for decathletes from the novice to national class range:

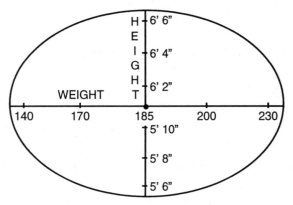

Average Size 6' 0", 185 lbs.

Like his training decisions, height and weight are a decathlete's compromise. Athletes who are tall have a leverage advantage in the throwing events and a high center of gravity for the hurdles and high jump. On the other hand, tall athletes have a more difficult time unwinding from starting blocks and staying within the throwing rings.

Heavier athletes obviously have more bulk to push the weights. For running and jumping events, their bulk is a disadvantage. The pole vault and 1500-meter run are particularly difficult for heavier athletes. Youngsters should not be concerned with height and weight; nature will take care of both.

One game some decathlon fans play is to assign points on a per pound basis. Just divide the best score by the decathlete's weight. Anything over 45 points per pound is exceptional. The results are interesting but the exercise is just for fun. The bottom line is clear. Although many coaches look for an ideal-sized decathlete, any size will do. Decathletes come in all shapes and sizes.

A QUICK LOOK AT THE EVENTS

Here is an overview of the 10 decathlon events:

100 Meters

This event measures basic leg speed. Each race/heat has between two and eight runners. Contenders push off a set of starting blocks in reaction to a starter's pistol and sprint for 100 meters, leaning at the finish line. The race can be timed with a hand-held stopwatch to 1/10th of a second, or by an automatic timing device that clocks to 1/100th of a second.

Long Jump

The athlete runs toward the landing area, plants his takeoff foot on an 8-inch "toeboard" and leaps into a sand-filled pit. The distance is measured from the print in the pit closest to the takeoff board. Speed and accuracy are secondary to leaping ability. Each athlete has only three chances and only the best jump counts in the scoring.

Shot Put

The shot put measures basic arm strength. Again, only the best of three attempts is used for scoring. The athlete puts (throws using an overhand pushing motion) a 16-pound iron ball so that it lands within a sector of 40 degrees. The throwing circle is 7 feet in diameter and made of concrete. Efforts do not count if the athlete oversteps the throwing circle or if the shot lands outside of the sector lines.

High Jump

In this event, the athlete approaches the bar and landing area, gathers himself and leaps (always off one foot) over a crossbar. The landing pit is usually made of foam rubber. The crossbar is raised, usually by 3 centimeters (approximately 1-1/4 inches), after each successful jump. The athlete is eliminated after three consecutive misses. The highest height cleared is used for scoring. The starting height of the bar is the lowest height that all competitors can clear.

400 Meters

A century ago, a quarter-mile race (440 yards) was deemed an endurance test. Today its metric equivalent is almost an all-out sprint. In this event, the athlete runs the entire distance in lanes. As in the 100-meter race, there are two to seven competitors. The 400 meters tests both speed and stamina and completes the first day's competition.

110-Meter Hurdles

The initial event of the second day demands speed and agility. The athletes sprint, not jump, over a series of ten 42-inch high barriers placed 10 yards apart. While sprinting, the athlete must stretch his stride pattern so he takes only three steps between hurdles. Hurdles may not be deliberately knocked down. (At the high-school level, hurdle height is 39 inches.)

Discus Throw

The discus weighs 2 kilograms (approximately 4-1/2 pounds) and is about 8-1/2 inches in diameter. Its shape has aerodynamic qualities. Again, only three tries are allowed. The athlete, while turning 1-1/2 times, must remain on an 8-foot 2-1/2-inch diameter concrete surface. The discus must land within a 40-degree sector. Only the best throw counts in the scoring.

Pole Vault

Technically, this is the decathlon's most difficult event. Grasping the upper end of a 14- to 15-foot fiberglass vaulting pole, the athlete races toward the pit, plants the pole in a takeoff box and swings himself up and over a crossbar, landing in a foam-rubber pit. Sound easy? It takes lots of practice.

Javelin

The javelin is a metal spear approximately 8 feet in length and weighing 800 grams (just under 2 pounds). At all levels except high school, the javelin must land point first within a 29-degree wide sector. Each athlete has three attempts and the best throw is scored.

1500 Meters

The final test is one of endurance, almost 4 laps around the 400-meter track. Rarely does the decathlete have the luxury of loafing during this event. He must give his best effort since, at approximately 6 points for every second, places, scores and records (personal or otherwise) are at stake.

WHAT ARE THE DECATHLON RULES?

Every decathlete should be familiar with track and field rules. With a few exceptions, the decathlon events follow the same rules as the individual events. The few exceptions are in the decathlon/multi-event section of rule books. Unfortunately, in the United States, there are four different rule books in use, depending on the level of competition.

- International meets (IAAF rule book)
- National/domestic meets (USATF rule book)
- Collegiate meets (NCAA rule book)
- High school meets (National High School rule book)

If you're competing, make sure you know which rules will be used for your decathlon. Don't despair! The differences in the rules are very minor. See "Important Addresses" for information about obtaining various rule books.

The following are a few of the differences between normal track and field rules and decathlon practices.

1. The decathlon must always be held on 2 consecutive days and contested in the following order:

First Day	Second Day
100-Meter Dash	110-Meter Hurdles
Long Jump	Discus Throw
Shot Put	Pole Vault
High Jump	Javelin Throw
400-Meter Dash	1500-Meter Run

The rule books also list the orders for other multi-event competitions including men's pentathlon, women's heptathlon and indoor multi-events.

2. An interval of at least 30 minutes should be allowed between the time one event ends and the next event begins. At the discretion of the games committee, this interval can be altered.

3. Each competitor will be allowed only three attempts in the long jump, shot put, discus throw and javelin throw.

4. It is recommended that fully automatic timing be used. If the meet is manually timed, each competitor shall be timed by three independent time-keepers. If the times differ, the median time shall be adopted. If for any reason only two register times, and they differ, the slower of the two shall be adopted as official.

5. In running events the competitor will be disqualified after three (NCAA, two) false starts.

6. In the high jump and pole vault, the games committee will set the starting heights and the bar will be raised in increments of 3 centimeters (for high jump) and 10 centimeters (for pole vault).

7. All measurements are metric. It is recommended that all measurements be made with a steel tape. Discus and javelin throws are measured to the least *even* centimeter. In the shot put, throws are measured to the least centimeter.

8. Sections and lane assignments for running events shall be determined by lot. No fewer than three competitors shall start in any section. In the final event, the 1500 meters, the leaders should run in the same heat. If athletes are grouped, the referee shall have the power to rearrange the groups.

9. Hurdles are run in adjacent lanes, except in collegiate meets where hurdles are placed in alternate lanes.

10. If a competitor fouls another competitor in any event, he shall lose the points gained for that event but shall be allowed to compete in succeeding events unless the referee deems that the loss of points is not a sufficient penalty.

11. Athletes must make an attempt at each event. This rule is designed to guarantee that the athlete intends to complete a decathlon and not just set records or get a workout in specific events. Athletes failing to start any event are

considered to have abandoned the competition, receive no final score and are not included in the final placing.

12. The event scores, cumulative scores and places shall be announced to the competitors at the completion of each event.

13. The winner of the competition is the athlete who has scored the highest number of points on the IAAF scoring tables (which are also included in the NCAA Rulebook). If there is a tie score, the athlete scoring the higher number of points in the most events shall be awarded the high place. If a tie still remains, then the competitor who has earned the highest number of points in any single event will be given the higher place. If the tie still exists, then the second-highest number of points is used, and so on. This rule applies to all decathlon competitions except those governed by NCAA rules. The NCAA does not break ties.

3

LET'S GET STARTED

The future decathlete is probably already a member of a track team, perhaps a community club or a high school or college team. He already has some experience with some events and an interest in others. The potential athlete may be introduced to the decathlete by his coach who senses that he has some talent to meet the demands of multi-events. If this is your introduction to the decathlon, consider yourself fortunate. The advantages of being introduced to the decathlon this way are numerous: a track and equipment provided by the club or school, an interested mentor to enter you in meets, and perhaps teammates to train with.

Unfortunately, it's not always that easy. "Decathlon talent" is not easily observable. Coaches may be too busy or uninterested. School facilities and equipment may be unavailable.

Fortunately, school authorities and coaches are rarely antagonistic. You're unlikely to have former NCAA decathlon champ Ed Miller's experience while he was preparing for the 1976 U. S. Olympic Trials. With the meet only a few weeks off, he was arrested for hopping a fence at a local college track to work out. Dissatisfied with his explanation, authorities handcuffed, fingerprinted and booked him. You probably won't have to go that far in defense of your devotion to the decathlon, but you can admire Miller's commitment. Miller has since become one of America's top decathlon coaches.

If your coach, parents or friends don't introduce the decathlon to you, then introduce it to them. If you are a member of the local track team, ask the coach for advice in preparing for the decathlon. If you are not part of a track and field program, contact the local coach, a parent, or a former decathlete.

Without being a pest, ask if he or she would take some time to help you with a few events. Don't ask your contact to coach you full-time; that's unrealistic. Just ask if he would be willing to observe you doing a few events, at a time that is convenient for him. If you are dealing with the local school coach, suggest convenient times like before or after formal practice sessions. The coach may allow you the use of equipment like shots, discs, vaulting poles or hurdles. Be polite and solicit information, perhaps names of other local decathletes. Some college athletes may be home for the summer. Some veteran athletes may be training nearby. Coaches will know the names and sites of a few meets, and perhaps even have entry blanks.

Many athletes don't know what a decathlon is until they find themselves competing in one. Enter a meet. Go and compete even if you have not prepared for some of the events. You'll meet other novices. You'll network. You'll get an idea about your own level of competency and how much training is necessary for success. You'll talk about the next meet. You'll be hooked.

Photo courtesy of the Dan O'Brien Youth Foundation

Age-group multi-events abound, providing young athletes the opportunity to develop good technique early in their careers.

The most commonly asked questions about getting started in the decathlon, especially from novices, are the following:

- How do I find out about decathlon competitions? What meets are available/open to me?
- How should I go about training for the decathlon?
- How do I find a coach?
- Where can I obtain a set of scoring tables?

This chapter answers the first question. The remaining questions are addressed in later chapters.

As recently as 1967 there were fewer than 10 decathlons held annually in the entire United States. Today the list exceeds 300. There are a number of reasons for the growing popularity. In 1970 the NCAA, following the lead of the National Association of Intercollegiate Athletes (NAIA) made the decathlon a scoring event in its national championship. College conferences, starting with the Intercollegiate Amateur Athletic Association of America (IC4A), followed suit. For the first time, college coaches began to recruit and train young men as decathletes and not as specialists. The popularity of the event mushroomed. Then, Bill Toomey's career proved that decathletes, if properly trained, could do more than one or two meets a season. The U.S.' 1980 Olympic boycotts put a temporary damper on increasing decathlon interest, despite Bruce Jenner's 1976 Olympic success. Corporate support helped rejuvenate decathlon activity. Visa became an event sponsor and Reebok featured two world-class decathletes, Dave Johnson and Dan O'Brien, in its 1992 multimillion-dollar advertising campaign. Currently, decathlon meets abound. You just need to know where to look. In the

United States, decathlon/multi-event opportunities are available in the following categories:

- Age
- Region
- Educational Level
- Ability
- Disability

While there is some overlap, this is a useful order for presenting competition information.

AGE

At the younger ages, there are three national programs for teenagers and subteen decathletes.

Youth Athletics Program

In recent years the national governing body for track and field, USATF, has formalized a program for youngsters. It offers a national championship meet and maintains national records for three categories. Although no decathlon is offered, abbreviated versions of multi-event competitions are offered, even to athletes under 10 years of age.

    I. Bantam (10 years and under): Triathlon (high jump, 6-pound shot put, 200 meters)

    II. Midget (11-12): Pentathlon (80-meter hurdles, high jump, 6-pound shot put, long jump, 800 meters)

    III. Youth (13-14): Pentathlon (100m hurdles, long jump, 4-kilogram shot put, high jump, 800 meters)

The 1996 National Youth Athletics meet will be held July 2-6 in Salt Lake City, Utah. For additional information about the Youth Athletics program, contact the chairperson of the Youth Athletics Committee of the USATF (see Decathlete's Address Book).

Junior Olympic Program

Since 1981 the USATF National Junior Olympic Program features decathlon competition at a national championship each July for the following two categories:

> I. Intermediate Boys (age 15-16)
>
> II. Young Men (ages 17-18)

In both categories, the events and scoring tables are standard, but the implements are lighter and the hurdles are lower (39 inches).

Each year approximately 25–30 athletes compete in each division and entry standards vary. The 1996 National Junior Olympic meet will be held in Houston, Texas.

The nation is divided into Junior Olympic regions and most regions (many are simply states) offer a regional qualifying meet, usually in June. If you do not know your regional Junior Olympic (JO) representative, contact the Youth Athletics Committee of the USATF (see Decathlete's Address Book). The USATF Press Information Office will know, by January 1 of each year, the dates, sites and name of meet directors for the national Youth Athletics and National Junior Olympic championships meets (see Decathlete's Address Book).

AAU Junior Olympics Program

There is a corollary national program called the AAU Junior Olympics that mirrors the USATF Youth/Junior Olympics program. Both groups run similar programs but the AAU deals with many other sports while the USATF deals only with track and field. The age groups and multi-events for both "Junior Olympics" programs are the same:

Division	Age	Event
Bantam:	10 & under	Triathlon
Midget:	11-12	Pentathlon
Youth:	13-14	16 Decathlon
Young Men:	17-18	Decathlon

There are 58 AAU associations and many offer meets at the association level. Athletes advance to regional meets and, in late July of each year, compete at a national AAU Junior Olympics competition. It is estimated that approximately 200-250 young men compete in AAU Junior Olympic multi-events annually. For more information, contact the national track and field director of the AAU Junior Olympics (see Decathlete's Address Book).

National Junior Program

Until 1972 the AAU Junior Championships were open to those who, regardless of age, had not won a national (AAU) championship, foreign championship or collegiate (NCAA, NAIA, IC4A) title. Pan American and Olympic team members were also ineligible. The first U.S. Junior Championship was conducted in 1900 and the eligibility rule held until 1972. Today the United States uses the standard international definition of *junior*:: athletes must be at least 14 and cannot reach age 20 in the year of competition.

Every year the USATF conducts a National Junior Championship meet, usually in the third week of June. There are no regional junior meets. Rather, athletes qualify for this competition by meeting a standard sometime during the spring season. Decathletes (who may either be college freshmen or high school athletes—as long as they do not turn 20) must meet a minimum qualifying score. Recently, they could meet the standard by scoring 6000 points with high school implements/hurdles or 5950 points using the international (college) implements. Each year the standards are adjusted slightly. Approximately 10-20 decathletes compete annually.

Every even-numbered year (1996-98-2000) the top two finishers qualify to represent the United States at the World Junior Championships. The 1996 World Junior Championship will be held in Sydney, Australia. Every odd-numbered year (1995-97-99) the top two finishers represent the United States at the Pan-American Junior Championships. The 1995 Pan-American Junior Championship was held in September in Santiago, Chile. In recent years, additional international competition has been provided to the top junior decathletes.

Masters and Veterans Programs

The fastest growing U.S. track and field activities are the masters and veterans programs. A masters competitor must be at least 40 years of age (there is a sub-masters level beginning at age 35). Veterans compete in age groups of 5 years (for example, 40-44, 45-49, 50-54, etc.) and today there are decathletes over the age of 90 still competing.

Every season the USATF conducts a National Masters Track and Field Championship that includes a decathlon. In 1996 it will be held in Spokane, Washington, and in 1997, it will take place in San Jose, California. National indoor and outdoor pentathlon meets are also offered.

The governing body for veterans affairs is the World Association of Veteran Athletes (WAVA). It sponsors a World Veterans Championship every odd-numbered year. The 12th WAVA World Championship will be hosted in Durban, South Africa in 1997. These are popular affairs. In 1989 the world meet was conducted in Eugene, Oregon, and it drew 123 decathletes.

There are also a number of regional veteran meets. The most popular are held in Lincoln, Nebraska, every summer and Thomasville, North Carolina, every fall.

As the ages increase, lower hurdles (for example, 39 inches at age 40, 36 inches at age 50) and lighter implements are used.

For scoring the decathlon, WAVA adopted age-graded tables in 1989. These tables use a series of age factors and age standards which take into consideration that a person's athletic performance declines with age. The factors compare performances over the years and, when applied to the IAAF decathlon scoring tables, offer a more meaningful score. They can be obtained from a very helpful monthly newspaper entitled, *National Masters News* (see Decathlete's Address Book). *National Masters News* (NMN) is indispensable for veteran athletes since it contains meet schedules and results.

One decathlete you'll meet if you take up the veteran's decathlon challenge is Rex Harvey, an engineer and former Air Force officer. Harvey began competing in 1965 and has completed so many decathlons that he'll soon be the first athlete in history to amass more than one million career points. He has been the WAVA world champion on several occasions and is always active on U.S. and WAVA multiple event committees. Another helpful contact is Barbara Kousky, chairperson of USATF Masters Track. To contact Rex Harvey and Barbara Kousky, see the Decathlete's Address Book.

Finally, for those interested in statistics, *National Masters News* and *Track & Field News*, both make available "Masters' Age Records." This annual booklet lists men's and women's world and U.S. age bests for all track and field events, age 35 and up.

REGIONAL PROGRAMS

The nation is divided in a number of ways by the USATF Association, by states, and by region of the country.

State Associations

USATF (formerly AAU and TAC) divides the nation by association districts, most of which conduct an outdoor track and field championship. For example, the Potomac Valley Association of USATF conducts track and field events in the Washington, D.C., Maryland-Northern Virginia area. Some associations conduct a decathlon with their annual meet, some conduct it separately and some ignore the multi-events. Currently, about a dozen associations annually offer a decathlon.

Contact your local association for a schedule of meets. If you don't know the association director in your area, contact Curtis Stitt, chairman of USATF's Associations Committee and he will be able to supply you with a list of all the associations and the names, address and phone numbers of all directors (see Decathlete's Address Book).

State Games

In the 1980s a wave of mini-Olympic affairs, conducted on a regional basis, swept the nation. Encouraged by the success of the Florida Sunshine Games, the New York Empire State Games and Pennsylvania's Keystone State Games, 35 states now offer athletic contests, usually during a one-week period in mid-summer. All offer track and field events and about half offer decathlons. Some, like New York, even have regional qualifying meets with decathlons. These are terrific developmental meets for college and high school athletes, who are constantly looking for summer meets.

They are normally conducted on the campus of a large college or university. You'll need to contact your state government (many are run out of the Governor's office) to find if a decathlon is offered. As of early 1995, the following states conduct summer games:

Alabama	Alabama Sports Festival	late June
Alaska	Greatland Games	late August
Arizona	Grand Canyon Games	late June
California	California State Games	mid August
Colorado	Cororado Sports Council	late June
Connecticut	Nutmeg Games	late July
D.C.	Capital Games	late June
Florida	Sunshine State Games	early July
Georgia	Georgia State Games	late July
Idaho	First Security Games	early July
Illinois	Prairie State Games	mid July
Iowa	Iowa Games	early August
Indiana	White River Park State Game	mid July
Kansas	Sunflower State Games	late July
Kentucky	Bluegrass State Games	late July
Massachusetts	Bay State Games	mid July
Minnesota	Star of North State Games	late June
Mississippi	State Games of Mississippi	early July
Missouri	Show-Me State Games	late July
Montana	Big Sky State Games	mid July
Nebraska	Cornhusker State Games	mid July

New Jersey	Garden State Games	early July
New Mexico	New Mexico State Games	early June
New York	Empire State Games	early August
North Carolina	State Games of North Carolina	late June
North Dakota	Prairie Rose State Games	late July
Ohio	Ohio Games	mid July
Oklahoma	Sooner State Games	mid June
Oregon	State Games of Oregon	early July
Pennsylvania	Keystone State Games	early August
Tennessee	Tennessee Sportfest	late June
Texas	Games of Texas	late July
Utah	Utah Summer Games	mid June
Virginia	Commonwealth Games	mid July
Wisconsin	Badger State Games	late June
Wyoming	Cowboy State Games	early June

EDUCATION LEVEL

In Europe, clubs and municipalities own and manage the track facilities. In America, the school systems (high school, junior colleges, college and universities) control the facilities. A majority of U.S. high schools have track and field teams and most have their own tracks, complete with jumping pits, throwing circles, hurdles and other equipment. Short of building your own track and field, any use of facilities and equipment for decathlon training and meets must be done with the cooperation and support of the schools and their coaches.

High School Decathlons

The decathlon is not a common event at the high school level, but it is gaining popularity and support. In 1994, 13 states offered state high school decathlon championships. Although the other 37 states did not, many state high school associations are beginning to offer a decathlon either as an invitational in the middle of the spring season or as a championship event its end. One stumbling block is that the javelin is not contested in some states Consequently, authorities are reluctant to offer an event that includes it. Some states have overcome this complication by offering a javelin clinic or instruction (including safety procedures) as part of the decathlon event, usually immediately before it. Signed waivers are also used.

Photo courtesy of the Dan O'Brien Youth Foundation

More than a dozen states offer a high school championship decathlon.

Some states offer a decathlon with a substitute for the javelin event. Alabama, Arkansas and Tennessee substitute the triple jump. The states that offered a high school decathlon in 1994 were the following:

Alabama	Florida	Vermont
Arkansas	Montana	Virginia
Arizona	New Hampshire	Washington
California	Tennessee	
Connecticut	Texas	

Contact your state high school association for more details. If a decathlon is not offered, you might encourage them to do so and even propose to organize it yourself. It's fun, and that's how most decathlons meets started. A few scholastic leagues also host a high school decathlon and there are at least five regional scholastic decathlons around the nation:

Brigham Young Invitational (held early May)	Great SouthWest Decathlon (held in late May)
Glendale (Ariz.) Invitational (early April)	New England High School (early July)
Ultimate Athlete Spring (late April)	

The latest exciting development at the scholastic level is the National High School Invitational Decathlon sponsored by the Dan O'Brien Youth Foundation and VISA. Scholastic decathletes are invited on the basis of their performances at the established meets listed above as well as their perceived potential. Held in Klamath Falls, Oregon, Dan O'Brien's hometown, the first two affairs (1994-95) were major successes. The meet is normally held during the first week of July. For more information, contact the Dan O'Brien Youth Foundation (see Decathlete's Address Book).

Many of today's decathletes started by doing a scaled down multi-event, perhaps a pentathlon. The National Indoor Scholastic Championship is held each March at the Carrier Dome on the campus of Syracuse (N.Y.) University. For more information and entry blanks contact Tracy Sundlun (see Decathlete's Address Book).

Junior College Decathlons

Many 2-year junior or community colleges offer track programs. The National Junior College Athletic Association (NJCAA) has conducted a decathlon as part of itsnational championships since 1973. Some of the junior college districts/states (for example, Arizona) also have a decathlon meet. Since the California Junior Colleges do not fall under the auspices of the NJCAA, they conduct their own championship decathlon (since 1970) every May, complete with North and South regional qualifiers each April.

Colleges/Universities

American decathletes get a lot of opportunities at the college and university level. Decathlon competitions strictly for college students date from the 1925 Penn Relays. However, it was 44 years later that collegiate organizations recognized the decathlon as a championship event. The progressive NAIA, a national organization of smaller colleges, initiated a national decathlon for its members in 1969 and Jeff Bennett of Oklahoma Christian College was its first winner. Indeed, many top decathletes came from smaller schools where they were in demand in a variety of events.

A year later, the NCAA made the decathlon a part of its national program both at the college division (smaller) and university division (larger) championships. Steve Gough (Seattle Pacific) and Rick Wanamaker (Drake) were the original titlists.

In 1974 the university division was renamed Division I and the College Division split into Divisions II (offering scholarships) and III (without scholarships). The automatic entry standards for each divisional meet are adjusted slightly each year. In 1995, the requirements were the following: I-7750 points; II-6850 points; III-6380 points. Provisional standards are also announced in order to fill a field of 16 to 18 athletes.

Numerous opportunities are available to the collegiate decathlete. Today more than two dozen collegiate conferences offer a decathlon, usually in May. The number of decathlons conducted as part of a collegiate invitational or relay meet now exceeds 75 annually. The collegiate decathlete may now be tempted to compete in too many meets, rather than too few.

In addition, the college conferences usually conduct an annual indoor pentathlon. The movement began with the IC4A in 1980. Now there are as many as 80 indoor pentathlons in the U.S. winter season. The NAIA and NJCAA offer the pentathlon as a championship event. The NCAA does not.

The current collegiate schedule places the U.S. National Championship immediately after the NCAA I Championship. This makes it extremely difficult for collegians to make the U.S. national decathlon teams since the top athletes must compete in two decathlons only 9 days apart. Consequently, some collegians are frozen out of later top competitions. More cooperation between the two groups is necessary to solve this problem.

The two top U.S. students are eligible to represent the United States at the Universaide, the World University Games, conducted in August/September of each odd-numbered year (1995-97-99).

ABILITY

American decathletes' ability ranges from the mediocre to the elite levels. At the lower range, scores of 4000 and 5000 are common. The national level requires 7000 points while scores in excess of 8000 points are world class. Annually about 70-100 athletes score more than 7000 nationwide and a dozen or so usually surpass 8000.

Open Meets

Qualifying for some meets requires a certain score, while other meets are open. In open meets, it is not unusual for final scores to vary by 3000 points. Finding an open meet for the beginner has, at times proved frustrating. It may require a systematic search and you may have to travel. Investigate the summer decathlons, state games and USATF district meets.

Many meets conduct several divisions: college, junior college, high school and open. A good beginner's meet is held every December at California State University at Long Beach. Nearly 100 athletes compete in five divisions. There are no entry standards. The longest continuously running decathlons with reasonable standards are the Mount Sac Relays (started in 1960), held at Azusa Pacific University each April, and the Eastern Championship (1968), now conducted at George Mason University in Fairfax, Virginia. Hint: one way to gain acceptance at some meets is to bring along some officials.

Sub-Elite Meets

This is a new term for decathletes who score over 7000 points during the spring season but are unable to meet the high standard necessary to compete in the U.S. nationals (usually in the 7750- to 7800-point range). Once the spring season ends, many of these decathletes lack high-level competitions. USATF, in cooperation with VISA and a nationwide health service, HealthSouth, have sponsored a national Sub-Elite Championship in mid-July at the University of Arizona in Tucson. The top finishers earn a spot on a U.S. team which meets a Canadian national team in a dual meet.

Elite Meets

The U.S. has held a National (AAU, TAC now USATF) Championship virtually every year since 1915. Either Dave Johnson or Dan O'Brien has won every U.S. title since 1989. The standard entry score is high (7750 points for 1995) and is fast approaching 8000 points. The standard to compete in the 1996 U.S. Olympic Trials decathlon is 8000 points.

Photo courtesy of Millsport

Elite-level decathlons abound. Houston native Drew Fucci was the 1995 U.S.O.C. Olympic Festival champion.

The top three finishers normally qualify for a major international competition via the U.S. Championship. Presently, the international calendar offers Olympic Games every fourth year and Pan American Games every pre-Olympic year. The IAAF World Championship takes place every odd-numbered year and the Goodwill Games every even-numbered non-Olympic year. For example:

1995	Pan American Games, Mar del Plata, Argentina
1995	IAAF World Championship, Göteborg, Sweden
1996	Olympic Games, Atlanta, Georgia
1997	IAAF World Championship, Athens, Greece
1998	Goodwill Games, New York

There are also two major international invitationals that attract the world's best decathletes. Every American elite decathlete should try to compete, at least once in his career, in Götzis, Austria, in late May. Set in the Austrian Alps near the Swiss border, the Götzis decathlon meeting is a quality affair with large, friendly crowds and spectacular scenery. Several world records have been set there. It is worth the trip.

In September, the international decathlon invitational meet DecaStar invites the top dozen decathletes worldwide to Talence, the wine country of Southwestern, France. Dan O'Brien set his current world record there. Both Götzis and Talence may soon become part of a decathlon Grand Prix circuit. Unfortunately for American decathletes, the U.S. nationals and Götzis are but two weeks apart, making for a demanding double.

The goal of representing your nation in an international championship is incentive enough for the hours, weeks, and years of training. Uncle Sam's decathletes have had a good deal of success in recent years, winning the past three World Championships, the past two Goodwill Games, the most recent Pan American Games and a bronze medal at the 1992 Olympic Games in Barcelona.

VISA, USA Decathlon Team

In early 1990, VISA announced its backing of a Gold Medal Athlete Program and conducted its first decathlon training clinic at San Francisco State University. It featured the Sports Science Division of the U.S. Olympic Training Center from Colorado Springs in which decathletes were videotaped, tested and analyzed in a variety of events.

At the 1990 U.S. National Championship, the initial 10-man VISA, USA National Decathlon Team was selected. The top 10 finishers at each U.S. championship make up the VISA national team. VISA provided training stipends, travel allowances and coaching support for team members for one year.

The program was approved by the U.S. Olympic Committee and track's governing body, USATF. Since 1991 two clinics (spring and fall) are held annually. Athletes are provided physiological and psychological testing, training opportunities, nutrition advice and the expertise of the nation's leading coaches. The five living American gold medalists:

Bob Mathias	1948 and 1952 Olympic Champion
Milt Campbell	1956 Olympic Champion
Rafer Johnson	1960 Olympic Champion
Bill Toomey	1968 Olympic Champion
Bruce Jenner	1976 Olympic Champion

attend each clinic and provide much-needed experience and invaluable counsel for the team members.

Photo courtesy of Millsport

VISA, USA Inc. supports a national decathlon team that is
assisted by U.S. Olympic decathlon chamions (left to right):
Bruce Jenner, Bill Toomey, Rafer Johnson, Milt Campbell and
Bob Mathias.

VISA has also offered support for developmental
decathlon meets. For example, VISA conceived an
annual VISA CUP meeting, a dual team match
between the United States and Germany, which itself
has a national club, Team Zehnkampf. The team's
permanent mentor is former decathlete Harry Marra
(former coach at San Francisco State). Princeton's Fred
Samara, a 1992 U.S. Olympic coach and Olympian is
also a vital factor.

The decathlon is the very first track event to have
corporate support. VISA's objective has been to keep
outstanding athletes training in their post collegiate
days. With so many recent international victories, the
world record returning the United States, and a slew

of 8000 scores, the program has been highly successful.

INDIVIDUALS WITH DISABILITIES

There is a variety of multi-event opportunities for the handicapped athlete. The organizations base their rules on official USATF rules, making modifications only as necessary. A USATF Competition Rule Book may be obtained by contacting USATF (see Decathlete's Address Book).

Deaf Athletes

Deaf athletes have made remarkable progress in recent years. Andrew Herman, son of 1964 U.S. Olympic decathlete Paul Herman, has scored more than 7000 points and is the current American Deaf Recordholder. Another impressive indication of deaf decathletes' capabilities has been the recent performance of Australia's Dean Smith, who competed in the 1992 Barcelona Olympic decathlon and placed 19th with 7703 points. He has a lifetime best of 7964 points. Deaf athletes use the regular IAAF scoring tables. However, instead of listening for the starter's pistol, deaf athletes watch the pistol, using its smoke as their signal.

Every four years the International Games for the Deaf (which includes a decathlon) is contested and U.S. teams have fared well. Selection trial meets are conducted. For more information, contact American Athletic Association of the Deaf (AAAD, formerly DAFUS) in the Deacathlete's Address Book or your state School for the Deaf.

Gallaudet University in Washington, DC, has a long-established record of track and field accomplishments. Gallaudet's outstanding coach, Tom Berg, is now retired, but for years he worked tirelessly to put his college on the track map. As a result, Gallaudet's track program is now a model of what deaf athletes (including decathletes) can accomplish. Recently, Don Boyer, the Middletown High School track coach in Western Maryland, has served as the decathlon coach for the internationally competing U.S. Deaf teams. For more information, you may want to contact either of these institutions in the Decathlete's Address Book.

Blind Athletes

There are currently three classifications of blind athletes, B1, B2, B3. These range from athletes who have no light perception in either eye (B1) to visual acuity of between 2/60 and 6/60 (B3). Annual competitions are conducted by the United States Association of Blind Athletes (USABA) and current USATF rules apply with certain modifications. The USABA offers pentathlon events for men and women. For men, the events are 100 meters, 1500 meters, long jump, javelin and discus. The International Blind Sports Association (IBSA) provides scoring tables. For mor information, these organizations are listed in the Decathlete's Address Book.

Special Olympics

Mentally handicapped athletes also have multi-event opportunities via the Special Olympics movement. Currently, a pentathlon is conducted at the quadrennial Special Olympic World Games and at annual national and regional Special Olympics competitions.

The Special Olympics pentathlon is the first day of the decathlon: 100 meters, long jump, shot put, high jump and 400 meters. It is recommended that the Special Olympics pentathlon be conducted over two days, with the first three events held on the first day and the remaining two events on the second day. Several years ago, I wrote the Special Olympics pentathlon scoring tables. They are printed in the Special Olympics Track and Field Handbook and available from the Special Olympics Director of Track and Field (see Decathlete's Address Book).

Calendar Recommendations

As mentioned earlier, moving the USATF national competitions back a few weeks would take care of the collegian (NCAA) problem and give American decathletes an opportunity to compete at Götzis and a chance at IAAF Grand Prix rewards. One proposal is that the United States combine its elite, sub-elite and junior national meets, for both decathlon and heptathlon, in a multi-event festival in late June. Other nations do this successfully as the large crowds and big scores demonstrate. Another benefit is that the entire multi-event community would be together once per year.

In the meantime, two track calendars are available. Every January I publish an annual decathlon calendar. Although not perfect, it lists dates, sites, contacts, and phone numbers of over 150 U.S. multi-event meets. It could be useful at a variety of levels in planning your competition schedule.

The USATF publishes an excellent Annual Athletics Calendar. available from its Press Information

Department. For either of these calendars, see Decathlete's Address Book.

START A DECATHLON MEET...

Even with decathlon opportunities available at a variety of levels, it is still possible that the budding decathlete will be in need of meets. Decathlon meets are hard to find in late summer and early fall (when weather is ideal). Also, many meets are closed to collegians or have entry standards. What can you do? I suggest that you start a decathlon meet....

You'll need a facility and equipment, a half dozen athletes, a handful of experienced officials, a scoring table and lots of energy. If you do not have experience organizing a decathlon, don't worry. No one else does, either. Your meet will be as official as necessary. Every meet had to start sometime. Who knows? Your meet may become an annual affair and, like most others, a labor of love by those who organize them. The athletes will appreciate your efforts and will return either to compete or officiate in the future.

Don't worry about making mistakes. Snafus occur even at national championship meets. Just do it. Good luck.

4

CLOTHING & EQUIPMENT

Apparel for Training

The most important consideration when selecting training attire is comfort. It is not necessary to wear the latest in track fashion or the most expensive shoes. It is worthwhile to invest in a few items for comfort. Let's take a closer look at what you'll need as you head out to the track.

Gym Bag

Purchase a roomy gym bag. Decathletes lug around lots of equipment and clothing. The more events you are practicing or the more variable the weather, the bigger the tote you'll need. At the track don't leave clothing or equipment lying around. If you are not using your equipment, place it in your bag to keep it in good condition.

Shoes

Decathletes use a lot of footwear. A basic pair of well-supported running flats is your most important investment. After all, you'll be in them more than any other shoe, so look for the essentials: comfort, stability, support. Your distance training, conditioning, general aerobic (non-sprint) running, warmups and warmdowns, even some weightlifting, will likely be done in these shoes. Since half of all decathlon injuries are foot related, obtain a decent pair. Even when the heels or soles wear out, shoe repair shops can rebuild them inexpensively.

A pair of running spikes (running surface determines spike length) is worth its weight in gold. They may not be inexpensive, but you'll use them for sprint, hurdle and even vault training and competition. If you also long jump in them, make sure they are reinforced and strongly stitched at the toe. Don't use them for long jumping if they're not designed for that purpose. Obtain a pair of long jump spikes.

As you become more proficient in each event, specialty shoes will make sense. Do not purchase a pair of javelin boots before you have had lots of javelin training. Putting an expensive pair of javelin boots on a weak thrower is like using a costly pair of skis on the beginners' slope.

Always bring all the shoes you'll need and at least two pairs of socks for each training session.

Shirts/Shorts

Next on the essentials list are proper fitting shirts and shorts. During practice sessions, these have nothing to do with fashion. Keep half a dozen or more tee shirts handy. You'll be surprised how fast you can go through them. The sleeve length is up to you. If sleeves get in the way of performing throwing events or the weather is hot, use a sleeveless shirt or singlet.

Photo courtesy of Millsport

Comfortable clothing is important.

Singlets should fit snugly. Comfort is crucial. Wear whatever feels comfortable and don't let your attire get in the way of performing the events. Extra long tee shirts and shorts, while fashionable for basketball, are clumsy and only get in the way of decathlon training. The same goes for running shorts. Lightweight nylon shorts are inexpensive and durable. Many decathletes opt for spandex running tights.

Sweatsuit

If the weather is cool, take along a sweatsuit. An inexpensive sweatsuit is invaluable, escpecially if you're just getting started. Most sporting goods stores offer a good selection.

Rain Gear

The use of a two-piece rainsuit is guided by the weather in your area. If you run in raingear, make sure that it fits loosely and is comfortable.

Jewelry

It is advisable to leave your jewelry at home. If you wear a nice watch, you may want to purchase an inexpensive sports watch (the kind that can time laps and intervals) to wear around the track. For safety, avoid wearing rings or necklaces.

Sunglasses

These, on the other hand, are often recommended. If you wear them in meets, wear them in practice sessions.

Equipment for Training

In the vast majority of cases, you will be a member of a track team and have access to the team's equipment. Virtually all the equipment you'll need is standard at most track and field facilities...hurdles, starting blocks, crossbars, pits, and throwing implements.

If you have permission to train at a track where you are not a student, you may need to bring equipment that is not readily available. This may include shots, disci, javelins vaulting poles and more. Is your gym bag getting heavy?

Before you leave a school's track program (either permanently or perhaps just for the summer months), find out if there is any equipment that the program can spare: an old vaulting pole, a broken discus, a worn out javelin. Eventually, you may need to purchase some equipment.

This equipment is not inexpensive. Local sporting goods stores do not usually stock these items and they'll have to be ordered. First consult the local track coaches—they always seem to have desks littered with these catalogs.

Disci, Javelins, and Vaulting Poles

Ask for advice and order with prudence. You won't need a heavy, 16-foot fiberglass vaulting pole if you can barely clear 11 feet. The top of the line javelins are of little use to someone throwing 100 feet.

After the implements arrive, take proper care of them. Find a special storage area out of the way of family traffic. Poles and javelins should *always* be in carrying cases when not in use. You want to prevent someone from stepping on the unprotected pole and cracking it. Fiberglass vaulting poles should lie flat when not being used; they should not be stood up. Transporting them will be your biggest headache. Airlines are famous for handling vaulting poles. More than one airline employee has sawed a pole in half to make it fit into a cargo bin!

Photo courtesy of Victah Sailer

At the higher levels of competition, decathletes use their own vaulting poles.

A good discus should last years. Keep it clean. Avoid nicks by keeping it away from concrete. *Only* throw your discus on a grassy landing area. Keep it in a leather carrying case. In most meets, you'll be able to use your own throwing implements. At the very highest levels, the Olympic Games and World Championships, the meet organizers will supply all throwing implements. In all cases, you'll need to use your own vaulting poles.

Other Items

For practice sessions, bring along an old towel (to wipe off throwing implements), a spiked marker (for long jump and pole vault runway marks), some adhesive tape, extra spikes and spike wrench, small first aid kit and a water bottle. Bring sunscreen if the weather is hot. Many decathletes use sun protection because of the amount of time they spend outdoors.

Now it's time to grab your cap (for shade) and gym bag and head to the track. The next chapter discusses what to do when you get there.

Apparel & Equipment for Competition

The decathlete must feel confident in his meet preparation. Knowing that he can be self-sufficient for the two days on the field is integral to a a good mental attitude. Whatever the weather, schedule or situation, the decathlete must have enough clothing and equipment to survive both the small problems, like loosing a spike, to the large ones, like breaking a vaulting pole.

Consult a checklist several days before the competition so that you have time to prepare or replace items.

By circumventing last-minute emergen-cies, you'll stay focused on the competition itself. Pack your bag the day *before* the meet and check each item again. The following is not an exhaustive list of what you need to pack, but it is a useful starting point.

CHECKLIST

Throwing implements (if not provided)

vaulting poles (most decathletes bring two or more)

folding chair (preferably with a low base)

umbrella (the larger the better)

Bag:

    measuring tape (for high jump, long jump, pole vault steps)

    markers (long jump and pole vault)

    several towels

    small first aid kit

    adhesive tape

    drinks and snacks

    two pairs of socks for each day

    two pairs of shorts

    two singlets

    two or three tee shirts

    more drinks and snacks

    sweatsuit

    rainsuit

    running spikes

    extra shoelaces

    event shoes (javelin, long jump, throws, high jump)

    hat or cap

    extra spikes and spike wrench

    sunscreen

    sunglasses

    headset and audio tapes

Knowing that you have conscientiously outfitted yourself with all the practical requirements of a decathlon gives you a confident frame of mind. Now all you must deal with are the 10 events. One final suggestion: You might want to pack a conversion table if you are unfamiliar with the metric system. Try to stay away from the scoring tables during the meet—too many athletes run to the tables after each event. Scoring is not your job. You need to concentrate on *doing* the events, not fretting about the scores.

5

DECATHLON TRAINING

Overview of Training

Before discussing specific training needs and training for individual events, it's essential to have a good understanding of the basic concepts underlying training in general:

- Recovery
- Balance
- Technique

Coach and athlete alike must understand that improvement in athletic performance is the result of both training and *recovery*. Hard training alone simply fatigues the body. The body's natural response to hard training is to rebuild weary muscles so that they become stronger than before. This rebuilding is done in the recovery phase of training. The length of the recovery phase depends on the amount of stress placed on the body during training.

The amount of physical work a young athlete can handle will be unique to the individual and depend on factors such as age, physical development, training background and work ethic. All must be taken into account in arranging a training program for an event as rigorous as the decathlon. Please remember to build recovery and rest (track's R&R) into the training schedule. It makes no sense to do a workout so strenuous that you are unable to train the next day.

Successful decathlon performance is a balanced effort. Therefore, *balance* in decathlon training is an ideal which needs careful and diligent planning. Decathlons are rarely won with one or two terrific events. They are certainly lost by one poor one. Balanced training requires a long-term commitment. Afterall, training for many of the decathlon events cannot take place simultaneously. The shot put, with its focus on power, and the 1500-meter run, requiring endurance, demand different types of training. The world's best shot putter does not need much endurance training. Conversely, developing endurance capacity does not require shot put drills. However, to become a multi-event athlete, some of both forms of training are desirable. Balance in training seeks a compromise between the two.

Perfect balance, though, is not the goal. For example, receiving the same number of points in each event is not a winning decathlon strategy. Scoring the maximum number of points is the goal. Remember the goal and don't lose sight of it. To better understand balance in training, consider the following potential "disaster events." Spills are frequent in the hurdles. Occasionally decathletes fail to clear the opeining height in the pole vault. It is not uncommon for the discus to land outside the sector in all three throws. All three instances result in a zero score. The first priority in training, then, should be to practice for dependability and confidence in these events, even though other events might be weaker.

Photo courtesy of Millsport

Young decathletes study pole-vault technique with Washington StateUniversity's coach, Rick Sloan, 1968 Olympic decathlete.

Finally, sound *technique* should be given primary emphasis in training, especially at the beginner's stage. Experience will enhance a young decathlete's speed, power and endurance. Flawless technique does not occur naturally. Sam Adams, the long-time track coach at the University of California at Santa Barbara put it this way: "The decathlon is the art of executing correctly." Many decathletes have eliminated themselves by throwing the discus outside the throwing sector, crashing down the hurdles, or missing low heights in either the high jump or pole vault—all for a deficiency in technique. A lot of technique is developed in the early teen years, as early as junior high school. Technique should be biomechanically sound. Otherwise, it needs to be unlearned, then relearned. This is time consuming and disrupting. Ken Doherty, Ph.D., author of *Track and Field Omnibook*, observes that for athletes who intend to make a career of the decathlon, no-learning is far better than learning poor technique.

The Fundamentals of Training

A sensible decathlon training program includes the following six elements:

Technique

The goal here is to find a simple, mechanically sound technique suited to the athlete. The greatest emphasis on technique should come in the earlier years when motor patterns are developed.

Speed

Many decathlon events are directly related to speed and speed training can be carried out year round. The intensity of the drills and workouts become more intense during in-season and in preparation for competitions. A series of sprints over 30, 60, 100, and 150 meters are common. Use adequate rest before the next sprint. Sprint form drills and practicing the start are also crucial.

Speed Endurance

This applies mainly to 400-meter training, but also to both the 1500 meters and 100 meters. The emphasis is, with good sprint form and body carry, to maintain the developed speed over longer distances. Various combinations of runs at 200, 250, 300, 400, 500 and 600 meters can be used.

Strength Training

Early in a decathlete's career a general strength training program using traditional weightlifting exercises should be emphasized. Olympic lifts like the snatch and clean and jerk, and power lifts like a bench press and half-squat, can be used. These workouts increase overall body strength. The novice or beginner decathlete may start by limiting his general strength training to a circuit on a Universal Gym or similar apparatus.

Specific strength training is aimed at developing power in throwing, jumping and running. These are dynamic exercises that attempt to imitate the event movements. Medicine ball drills, bounding, hopping and jumping over hurdles are all examples.

General strength training should overshadow specific strength training in the early stages of a career. Once the athlete reaches a proficiency in most events, strength training can be split between general and specific. Never underplay the importance of general strength training. At the same time, don't overdo it. The idea with weightlifting is not to build bulk but to enhance strength. Decathletes don't enter Mr. America contests. They compete in decathlons. To do so successfully, their strength training must be a corollary to technique workouts.

A word of caution about weightlifting: Never lift alone. Always lift with a spotter, friend, another decathlete. This is important for safety and motivational reasons.

Endurance Training

The purpose of this type of training is to develop an aerobic base that enables the decathlete to run a solid 1500 meters and to have the stamina to endure the long hours of decathlon competition. Endurance training can be accomplished in the off-season by faithful and frequent runs of 20-30 minutes, perhaps three times a week. Adding a 20-30 minute Fartlek session once a week during the off-season is adequate. During the competitive season, several paced efforts at 800, 1000, 1100 or 1200 meters are advisable and good for confidence.

It is not necessary to become a distance runner. However, a national-class athlete in satisfactory condition should always be able to run the equivalent of a 5:00 mile (in other words, a 4:40 1500 meters). At 6 points for every 1-second improvement, the 1500-meter event can not be ignored.

Flexibility Training

Often overlooked, this is an important ingredient of training. It not only helps prevent injuries but also improves technique by allowing a greater range of motion. *Every* workout should be preceded by a 15- to 20-minute stretching session.

Training Cycles

Some decathletes like to use training cycles in which all the events are practiced. Common are 21-day, 14-day and 1-week cycles. These vary in intensity, depending on the time of year. In-season activities focus on refining speed, speed endurance and perfecting technique. Off-season activities feature more work with endurance and strength. All activities feature flexibility. Below is a sample 14-day cycle for a novice or veteran decathlete. It is a general plan. The seasoned decathlete would emphasize a more intense work load (longer workouts, heavier lifts, more repetitions, faster runs). Remember, this is just a sample and each decathlete needs to build his own training cycle.

Sample Training Cycle

For: In-season, competitive season

Length: 14 days

Level: Novice to Veteran

Day 1   Sprinting, Long Jump, Shot Put, evening strength

Day 2   Hurdles, Discus, Pole Vault, 400-meters training

Day 3   Weak events, evening strength

Day 4   Sprinting (starts), Shot Put, High Jump

Day 5   Hurdles, Pole Vault, Javelin, 400-meters training

Day 6   General strength training

Day 7   Rest

Day 8   Sprinting, Shot Put, High Jump, evening strength

Day 9   Hurdles, Pole Vault, Javelin, 400-meters training

Day 10 Long Jump, Shot Put, 1500-meters training, strength

Day 11 Hurdles, Pole Vault, 400-meters training

Day 12 Light warmup or general strength

Day 13 Competition in three to five events

Day 14 Rest

Note: in preparation for a decathlon on the 13th or 14th day of a 14-day cycle, the volume of work is reduced starting with day 8. On day 8 or 9, a fast 300 meters is advised. On days 9 or 10 some short sprint work is recommended. Days 11 and 12 should be light, perhaps some technique work or active rest (perhaps an easy bike ride or walk).

Sequence Training

You may have noticed that, in the sample training cycle above, many of the events are practiced in the order in which they competitively occur in a decathlon. The discus is practiced after the hurdles, and the pole vault after the discus, just the way they occur on competition day. This is called sequence training. The idea is to condition the body to move from one event to the next. For example, if your legs are always wobbly after the hurdles, it is important to simulate that feeling in practice by throwing the discus after a hurdles workout. This conditions the athlete to make the transition from one event to the next.

The late Estonian and Soviet decathlon coach, Fred Kudu, suggests that decathletes not be married to the concept of sequence training. For some athletes, it's useful. An important sequence within the training session themselves is most important. Train for technique and speed at the onset of the training session, with jumping in the middle and strength and endurance at the end of a session.

A Few Notes About Training for the Novice

Novice decathletes vary greatly in age, ability, interest and experience. The problems faced by a 15-year-old high school sophomore, a 21-year old college junior and a 44-year-old Masters decathlete will be different. One may have years of track and field experience, another little to none. Their basic goal is still the same: to complete all 10 events to the best of their abilities and with the hope of competing in future decathlons.

Because of the demands of the decathlon, the training load is heavy. To prevent injuries and maintain a fresh attitude, I offer a few training tips:

- Plan an adequate amount of rest. Plan rest days, or easy days. The only things you accumulate by trying to work out without rest are injuries.

- Have at least one training partner. Few great decathletes train alone. It's safer and more fun. Never, *never* vault alone.

- Vary your training sites. Occasionally go to another track, golf course, or weight room. With all the demands of decathlon training, it is easy to fall into a tedious routine.

- On any given day, do sprint and technique work before any speed endurance workout. Endurance and power training should be done at the end of the session, not before. Don't do a long run or a weightlifting session, then come to the track to sprint, vault or hurdle. You're likely to windup injured. Sprint and technique work must be done while you are fresh.

- If you have advanced to the stage of using a training cycle (discussed above), technique work should follow a rest day or easy training day. Speed and speed endurance should be placed in the middle of the cycle, with endurance and strength work place near the end.

- Don't ignore weak events.

- Don't be afraid to experiment.

- Don't sacrifice training for indoor or early season results.

- Sometimes less is more. If you are tired, err on the conservative side and call it a day. The number of injuries caused by and to tired decathletes is almost epidemic. You have heard and seen it before: "Let's do one more repeat," or, "Why don't you take one more throw." Injuries result and careers are altered or ended by coaches who want you to train until *they* get tired. Set a predetermined number of efforts. Do them, then stop. Use common sense.

10. Keep records of your training session. A small log book or notebook will do. Notes will be valuable in the future for putting together a training regime or just to see what you did right before that big breakthrough.

Photo courtesy of Millsport

Training partners can offer support, advice, competition and sympathy.

For More Training Details

For viewpoints in this chapter I am indebted to Ken Doherty, Ph.D., whose *Track and Field Omnibook* is the bible for much track and field training. It should be consulted for more detailed aspects of training for each of the individual decathlon events. Dr. Doherty was an Olympic decathlon medalist, national decathlon champion, long-time coach at both Michigan and Pennsylvania, meet director of the Penn Relays and is the sport's most prolific writer. He is an inductee of the National Track and Field Hall of Fame.

I also drew upon the work of a pair of former decathletes regarding elementary training cycles. Gordon Stewart, former Canadian recordholder, and Vern Gambetta, former editor of *Track Technique*, wrote "Decathlon Training: From Beginner to Master." Please see "For Further Reading" for bibliographic information.

6

DOING YOUR FIRST DECATHLON

The beginner's first priority is to *complete* the entire 10 events. *Finish.* If you have any concern that you might not finish your first (or any decathlon), don't start. Instead, consider tackling a few one-day pentathlons (indoors or out) before going to a full decathlon.

The standard indoor pentathlon consists of 60-meter hurdles, long jump, shot put, high jump, and 1000-meter run. The outdoor pentathlon is also standard: long jump, javelin, 200 meters, discus, 1500-meter run. Even a triathlon, consisting of any run, jump or throw, (for example, hurdles, high jump, javelin) will be useful. Specifically, it's important to experience competition in the pole vault, hurdles, discus and javelin in the weeks prior to your first decathlon. These are troublesome and exacting events so, for psychological reasons, it's crucial to at least score in them before your first decathlon.

In your first decathlon, try to score some points, even a modest amount, in each event. To do this, it's necessary to have some sort of rough technique in the four aforementioned events. In the hurdles, try and establish three steps between hurdles for as long as possible. If you have to drop to five, so be it. The author recalls one high school athlete who alternated and took four strides between hurdles—this is not recommended. In the pole vault, use a short run, perhaps in the 10-to 15-stride range, with a low top-hand hold (9–10 feet). In the discus, adjust your starting position in the circle to ensure a fair landing. Finally, in the javelin, a short (perhaps 5- or 7-step), controlled approach will likely provide a decent throwing position and toss.

Photo courtesy of the Dan O'Brien Youth Foundation

In your first decathlon, it's important to score in every event.

On your first effort in the long jump, use a conservative approach in terms of steps to guarantee a legal mark. There is a good case for taking at least one jump at a low height in both the high jump and pole vault, regardless of your level of experience. You'll use little energy and any step problems can be resolved at a lower height. There is also the psychological satisfaction of clearing at least on height. At no time, when approaching personal record (PR) heights, should a decathlete pass a height.

In terms of the 1500 meters, even if you have little to no experience in anything longer than 400 meters, try to establish a 5-minute 1500 meter pace in the weeks leading up to your first decathlon. Repeat some occasional 400-meter runs in 80 seconds or 800-meter runs in 2:40. The author recalls a novice collegiate decathlete with 47-second 400 meter running skills. He ran the first 400 of a 1500 in 61 seconds, then spent the next 4 minutes running in sand. His was a short career.

Let's go to the first meet. Needless to say, you arrive with adequate shoes and clothing, having taken into account the possibility of bad weather. You have ample snacks and fluids. The decathlete must be self-sufficient in terms of equipment and supplies. Nothing must disturb your concentration.

Precede each event with a specific warmup: stretching, jogging, striding, sprinting, hurdling, jumping, throwing—whatever the event dictates. The warmup for the previous event does not serve for the following event.

Don't carry over failures from the preceding event. Only carry over successes. Forget the failures and get on with the next event.

Finally, stay off your feet when you're not warming up or competing. Part of the decathlon game is managing your energy.

Your first meet will be invaluable as a learniung experience, for evaluating strengths and weaknesses. One way to do so is to make notes of each meet. A simple notebook is sufficient to record your observations and results. Wait until the meet or day is over before writing down your comments. In the future they will be a useful resource. Here is a sample:

PERSONAL DECATHLON RECORD

Name of Meet:				
Site:		Date:		
This is my	decathlon;	PR score:		
Event	**PR**	**Performance**	**Points**	**Comments**
100m				
LJ				
SP				
HJ				
400m				
	1st day			
110mH				
Disc				
PV				
Jav				
1500m				
	2nd day			
Total Score:		Place:		Winner:

Perhaps that first record sheet will look like this:

PERSONAL DECATHLON RECORD

Name of Meet: *COUNTY CHAMPS*

Site: *Lakeland*   Date: *May 18-19, 1996*

This is my *1ˢᵗ* Decathlon; PR score: *None*

Event	PR	Performance	Points	Comments
100m	11.6	11.8	643	*Too nervous at start. Ran tight.*
LJ	20-8/6.30m	19-11/6.07m	602	*Missed board, other 19-11*
SP	32-7 1/2/9.94m	33-7 1/2/10.25m	501	*1st throw-BAM! Relaxed*
HJ	5-4 1/4/1.63m	5-5/1.65m	504	*Came in at 4-9. Jumped at every height. Satisfied.*
400m	55.9	57.1	512	*Went out too fast. Died Big Time*
	1st day		2762	
110mH	None	18.3	474	*Maintained 3 stride for 5 hurdles. Stumbled at 10th.*
Disc	96-5/29.40m	95-2/29.00m	445	*1st throw outside sector. 2nd slipped. Could be worse.*
PV	None	8-6 1/4/2.60	264	*Used 2 step approach, hung on*
Jav	126-10/38.66m	121-9/37.12m	401	*5 step approach. Windy Getting Tired.*
1500m	None	5:12.20	492	*Tried to stay with leaders. Last lap AGONY.*
	2nd day		2076	

Total Score: *4838*   Place: *5th*   Winner: *Massa/Clearview 5414*

This score of 4838 points is a good one. Why? Because the first success in the decathlon is to complete it. Don't dismay that the score is 4000 points shy of the current world record. Dan O'Brien, who holds that record, recorded a 4643 total in his very first decathlon as a Klamath Falls, Oregon, high school freshman. As you can see, he has made considerable progress. Bill Toomey's first decathlon in 1959 netted him just 5349 points. Nine years later, he was the Olympic champion and a year after that, the world-record holder with 8417 points. So you see, any score is a good one for your first decathlon. Just complete it. Toomey, now an articulate motivational speaker, likens starting the decathlon to looking up a long flight of steps. Climbing those steps won't be easy but you'll discover that the view at each new elevation gets better and better. This improvement produces satisfaction. "Don't put a lid on what you can achieve," says Toomey. "Just take one step at a time and use setbacks productively. Learn. The decathlon is like golf. Your next stroke could be your best one. And don't be overly concerned about how fast you move up those steps. Some guys are on escalators while others have to take it one step at a time." Learn from your first and each decathlon. Toomey concludes, "Every day in the decathlon you have a chance to be better than you've ever been before." Immediately after your first completed decathlon, you'll already be making plans for the next one.

Photo courtesy of the Dan O'Brien Youth Foundation

Personal record (PR) vault clearances occur frquently in early competitions.

7

NUTRITION, HEALTH HAZARDS, & FIRST AID

Nutrition

Diet significantly influences athletic performance. A decathlete's diet, both in terms of quantity and quality before, during and after both training and competition, will maximize results. The optimum diet for the decathlon is likely to have the following composition: carbohydrates about 60-70 percent of total energy intake, protein about 15-20 percent, with the remainder coming from fat.

Carbohydrates are sugars and starches found in grain and grain products (cereals, bread, rice, pasta), fruits, vegetables, milk and dairy products and many processed foods and drinks. *Proteins* are the body's building blocks needed for growth and repair of damaged cells. Proteins help digestion and fight infection. The major sources of protein are meats, fish, milk and dairy products, eggs and nuts. *Fats* are a concentrated source of food energy. They help build the body tissues and contain the fat soluble vitamins—A, D, E and K. Saturated fats are found in red meats, whole eggs, whole milk and milk products. Unsaturated fats are found in nuts and many vegetable oils. Although fat is essential in the diet, nutritionists recommend that fat provide no more than 10-20 percent of an athlete's energy intake. A note of caution: animal products (for example: red meat) are not the only sources of protein and fat. Some world-class athletes follow a low-fat diet composed mostly of plant foods.

We also need a wide range of vitamins and minerals in our diet. A varied diet can fulfill our normal requirements since vitamins and minerals are needed in small quantities. High-energy supplements may be valuable but are no replacement for an adequate diet. Water and fiber are also needed in our diet. Decathletes need to drink extra water.

Decathletes need more energy than the average person. The more active you are, the more energy you need. Decathletes use 5,000 or more calories a day. Where should this extra energy come from? Scientific research indicates that this extra energy should come from increasing carbohydrate intake rather than from more protein or fat.

A healthful diet provides the energy we need from the correct proportions of nutrients. A wide variety of foods and drinks ensures that we obtain all the vitamins and minerals we need.

Total energy intake must be raised to replace the energy drained during training. Decathletes should always monitor their body weight, body composition (percentage of fat) and food intake. From a nutrition standpoint, the decathlon is both a power and an endurance event.

Photo courtesy of Millsport

Proper nutritionhelps supply the power for the three throwing events.

Fluid intake is as important as the intake of carbohydrates and other nutrients. All body cells contain water. It accounts for 60 percent of body weight. Water cools the body, transports nutrients, and maintains blood volume. Dehydration causes the body to overheat. Even small, unreplaced fluid losses can impair performance. Decathletes should not wait until they feel thirsty before drinking. Athletes must drink *before* they feel thirsty. Because there is a premium on endurance, decathletes should drink water before, during and after both training and competition. Drink more than you think you should.

A quick word about alcohol: Although some find it enjoyable, consuming alcohol does nothing to prevent dehydration. Alcohol is a diuretic; it increases urine formation so that slightly more fluid is lost as urine than is consumed in an alcohol beverage. It therefore increases rather than decreases dehydration. Under no circumstances should a decathlete have alcohol in any form (not even one beer) during training or competition or between competitive days.

A word of caution about nutritional supplements: Many claim amazing results, but be suspicious. Most nutritional research does not support those claims. Unless there is a natural deficiency or the work load is abnormally high, athletes eating an adequate diet in terms of quantity and quality, will find little need for nutritional supplements.

Health Hazards

Athletes of all ages, and especially young and talented ones, are subject to an extensive assortment of influences. For many youngsters, the desire to accommodate external or internal pressures tempts them to adopt habits that can jeopardize their track careers, and their health.

Smoking More than a generation ago the Surgeon General warned all Americans of the health dangers of smoking. Smoking's damage to lungs, and its influence as a cancer agent, are overwhelming and undeniable. The initial reduction of lung capacity in a strong, young athlete may seem insignificant, and might be, if tobacco were not also an addictive drug.

For youngsters who intend to make a career of the decathlon, abstinence from cigarettes is an absolute.

There are world-class athletes (and decathletes) who smoke. I recall my amazement at a post-decathlon reception in the 1980s where numerous European decathletes were smoking. They claimed that, in their condition, smoking would have minimal influence on their conditioning/performance and that it was important to relax after a big meet. They are now retired from active competition...and still smoking. Be assured there are many alternatives to addictive drugs for unwinding!

Smokeless Tobacco National surveys warn us of the surprising increase of the use of smokeless tobacco by high school and junior high school students. As a college professor, I am distressed by the number of students who come to class displaying the smokeless tobacco habit. Perhaps this is caused by peer pressure or the desire to emulate professional athletes.

If you intend to compete in something as strenuous as the decathlon, put all notions of smokeless tobacco products aside. The health repercussions are numerous. Pouch tobacco has a typical sugar content of 35 percent. Soaking teeth in sugar greatly enhances the risk of cavities. Gum disease and tooth loss are not uncommon. The National Institute of Drug Abuse and the American Psychological Association both state that smokeless tobacco can result in a dependent habit. It is a myth that the use of smokeless tobacco will enhance an athlete's reaction time to the starter's pistol, but it is no myth that the use of smokeless tobacco can have long-term health implications.

Anabolic Steroids The use of steroid drugs, properly called anabolic-androgenic steroids (AAS), became prominent in the U.S. weightlifting community in the

Middle Atlantic states in the late 1950s and early 1960s. The purpose of AAS is to both enhance athletic performance and stimulate muscular development. There is some evidence to suggest that it does both, but at a heavy price to long-term health.

The consequences of steroid use are so appalling that they easily outnumber any possible performance benefits to the user.

In young boys the use of AAS can result in acne, overly developed breasts, hair loss and the yellowing of eyes. Body growth can be stunted. The American Sports Education Institute counsels that there are psychological effects to anabolic steroid use which may include any of the following: extensive mood swings from raging violence to depression, irritability, jealousy, delusions and damaged judgment.

Why anyone would risk any or all of the above disorders is a great mystery to sports observers. Yet track and field is still bedeviled by steroids and, in the United States, steroid use among youngsters, athletes and non-athletes alike, is extremely high, perhaps in the millions. Their desire for approval through muscular growth is serious indeed. A sizeable portion of young male users are non-athletes who simply want to look like Tarzan. It's estimated that the sales of illegal steroids in the United States (the substantial fraction via direct mail or gyms) now exceeds $400 million annually. As a nation, we will pay the price in health problems within the next generation.

The most widely publicized case of steroid misuse involved Canadian sprinter Ben Johnson who was divested of his 100-meter dash gold medal after failing a drug test at the 1988 Seoul Olympics.

Nationally and internationally, a number of decathlon men have been suspended for steroid use. Random, year-round testing at the elite levels is conducted both by the American federation, USATF, and by the International Amateur Athletic Federation (IAAF). Testing also occurs at the club level, at major meetings and is also conducted by the National Collegiate Athletic Association (NCAA). Today, at least in track and field, athletes run a heavy risk of being detected because of frequent out-of-competition testing. The highly successful VISA, USA Decathlon program, initiated in 1990, is a prime example of how its team members can be world-class decathletes and drug free.

Ethically, the use of AAS for muscle building or improved athletic performance is deplorable. It's incomprehensible that athletes would want, and the public accept, better performances through pharmacy. We do not want to see athletes become inhuman. To learn more about AAS and its effects, please see *Anabolic Steroids: Altered States*, by James E. Wright and Virginia S. Cowart.

Alcohol Many Americans make drinking beverage alcohol a part of their lives and do so in a responsible manner. For young track and field athletes, and decathletes in particular, the question of what to drink or *not* to drink figures prominently in their social lives. Alcohol's dehydrating effect on the body has already been noted. Additionally, alcohol is a depressant.

Partly in reaction to societal pressure, many youngsters, including athletes, drink immoderately. They run a high risk of alcohol-related problems, including drunk driving accidents. As long as alcohol is not part of training or competition, and done in moderation, its impact on a decathlon career will be minimal. The same cannot be said for any recreational drug usage. These have no place in sports. Remember, obey the law.

First Aid

Two important precautionary measures: First, before beginning training, the prospective decathlete should have a physical examination by a medical doctor. Second, always train with a partner so that someone will be available if an injury occurs.

Much of decathlon activity, both training and competition, is ballistic. This means that rapid, powerful movements are used. The physician will caution you about overwork and remind you that muscles need to be conditioned. Stress on body parts can result in injury. Some common injuries to decathletes are acute strains to:

Hamstrings muscles

Quadriceps muscles

Groin muscles

Knees (including hyperextension)

Ankles

Shoulder muscles

Sufficient stretching helps reduce your chances of injury. Stretch for 15–20 minutes before every training session. All muscles to be used should be stretched in a static fashion, holding the stretched position for at least 5-10 seconds. Avoid bouncing, jerking motions. Muscles are much like rubberbands. They must be slowly stretched, not yanked apart. Don't start your workout until you have completed the stretching phase.

Should an injury be sustained, apply ice immediately and rest the muscle. If the injury is serious, consult a physician.

Some athletic injuries are caused by a simple muscle imbalance, for example, between quadriceps and hamstrings. If one set of muscles is significantly stronger than another, muscle pulls will be common. Consult your coach and trainer about tests for muscle imbalance.

In most school situations a trainer is available to treat athletic injuries. However, if the athlete is training off-hours, off-season or without the supervision of a trainer, then a first aid kit should always carried to the training site, whether it be the track, a field, fieldhouse, or weightroom. The typical contents of a decathletes's first aid kit would include:

- Adhesive bandages of various sizes
- Adhesive tape (1- to 2-inches wide)
- Antibiotic ointment
- Bandaids
- Unbroken cold packs
- Elastic bandages
- Scissors
- Bottle of ibuprofin
- Towel
- Utility knife, for example, a Swiss Army knife
- Several quarters (emergency phone calls)

Your local pharmacy has all of the above items. Also, tape the athlete's insurance information and the phone numbers of physicians and emergency vehicles inside the first aid kit.

Always bring plenty of fluids to any training session or competition. A rule of thumb is to drink four 8-ounce cups of fluid for every pound of weight lost in exercise. There are many sport drinks available that replace lost salt, minerals and other electrolytes.

Serious injuries in the decathlon are uncommon but it is always better to be prepared. If you believe an athlete's injury to be serious, the following guidelines will help everyone:

Remain calm. Screaming will not help. It's hard to make decisions when you are upset. Moreover, your behavior may determine the reactions of others around you, including other athletes, officials, parents and spectators.

Don't move an injured athlete. This could compound the injury. If the athlete is unconscious, make him as comfortable as possible and send for immediate help. Whenever there is any doubt as the nature or extent of an injury, ask for emergency help.

Under no circumstances should the injured athlete be allowed to continue the training or competition. Rest is nature's remedy for most injuries.

Athletes and coaches must use common sense about athletic injuries. There is a tendency for athletes to try to return to training too soon after an injury. This increases the chance of a more serious injury and perhaps the loss of a season. For example, hamstring injuries normally sideline an athlete for 1–3 weeks, depending upon the injury's severity and response to treatment. Make sure the athlete has the whole range of motion and can train without pain before allowing him to compete. If there is a question, err on the side of caution.

For more information about the prevention and cure of athletic injuries, you can refer to many standard texts. One is *Sports Medicine: Prevention, Evaluation, Management and Rehabilitation*, by Roy and Irvin.

Chapter Acknowledgments

In the section on nutrition, I have relied on the conclusions of the International Scientific Consensus Conference on Foods, Nutrition and Sports Performance held in February, 1991, in Lausanne, Switzerland. I am indebted to earlier Guides in the USOC Sports Series, especially the *Basic Guide to Soccer* written by Joey Lorraine Parker, for my sections on both smokeless tobacco and anabolic steroids. For the section on First Aid I am indebted to Mr. Colin Provost, Trainer at Mount St. Mary's College, for his help in identifying common decathlon injuries.

8

DECATHLON SCORING TABLES

It has often been said that the most difficult thing about the decathlon is not *doing* the 10 events, but understanding the scoring tables. The difficulty lies in the scoring tables' subjectivity. The scores are, afterall, only arbitrary assignations of numbers to each athletic event. Fortunately, you don't need to understand them. Few people do. All sports have constants and the current IAAF scoring table is the decathlon's constant. Like 10-foot baskets or 90-foot basepaths, the table gives the decathlete a point of reference.

No matter what else is said about the construction of the table (and much is said), it is the same for everyone. In basketball, for example, despite their variations in size and skill, all players shoot at the same hoop. Muggsy Boggs and Shaquele O'Neal both aim at a 10-foot rim. In the decathlon, all competitors work with the same table. Even if you don't like the tables, a change in the IAAF scoring tables is as unlikely as raising the baskets to 12 feet so we may as well accept them.

Photo courtesy of Millsport

Always designate someone to keep the official score as scoring errors are common.

The construction of the scoring tables should have an impact on how the decathlete trains. Each of the event tables has slightly progressive slopes. That is, for each additional constant improvement in performance, more and more points are awarded. As in any economizing situation, the decathlete wants to maximize points given a fixed amount of resources, namely, time, skill, experience and work capacity. Each decathlete should examine his own capabilities and stage of development as well as the tables to determine which events he will stress in training. It's not effective for an athlete with great long-jump skills to train long hours to hone that event. He would receive just a few incremental points when he could have used a shorter period of time to pick up the same additional points in, for example, the 400 meters.

An athlete's stage of development is very important to consider. Athletes in their early years can easily pick up more than 150 points in the 400 meters by improving from 57.9 to 54.0. Add another 150 points by going from 5:05 to 4:40 in the 1500 meters. The 300 points can be produced without any improvement in skill. Indeed, the 1500 meters appears to be an event that pays big dividends for improved performance. Each additional 1-second reduction adds another 6 points to your score. Take advantage of it.

This strategy does not mean decathletes should ignore some events in favor of others. Reliance on scoring heavily in a few events no longer results in a decathlon victory. A balanced performance is the key since it is the balanced athlete who finds himself in less trouble if one of his events goes awry—especially if it is one of his better events. He will have other solid events to fall back on.

As a decathlon meet approaches, I recommend that athletes remain running sharp. There are big points to be gained by incrementally faster times and, conversely, lost if your speed is not sharp.

The decathlon events are measured and scored in meters. You'll need to become moderately familiar with the metric system because you cannot, for example, look up a 6-foot high jump in the IAAF tables. If you want to know the closest imperial conversion, you'll also need a conversion table. A high jump of 6 feet equals 1.83 meters. If you look up

1.83 meters in the scoring tables, you'll find that it is worth 653 points.

Below is a sample of what the international tables look like.

Men High Jump	
Metres	Points
1.89	705
1.88	696
1.87	687
1.86	679
1.85	670
1.84	661
1.83	653
1.82	644
1.81	636
1.80	627

The Scoring Tables are published by the IAAF but the easiest way to obtain a copy in the United States is via *Track and Field News*. Ask for *Scoring Tables for Men's and Women's Multi-Event Competitions*. The IAAF tables are also printed in the annual *NCAA Track and Cross Country Men's & Women's Rules*. Another very handy guide is *Track and Field News'* spiral-bound *Big Red Book*.. It contains a conversion table, an abbreviated set of scoring tables, and much more useful information. It is invaluable at decathlon competitions. See the Decathlete's Address Book.

Here is a summary of the scoring tables:

Event/Points	1000	900	800	700	600	500	400
100 Meters	10.39	10.82	11.27	11.75	12.26	12.81	13.41
Long Jump	7.76m	7.36m	6.95m	6.51m	6.06m	5.59m	5.09m
Shot Put	18.40m	16.79m	15.16m	13.53m	11.89m	10.24m	8.56m
High Jump	2.21m	2.11m	2.00m	1.89m	1.77m	1.65m	1.52m
400 Meters	46.71	46.19	50.32	52.58	54.98	57.57	60.40
110m Hurdles	13.80	14.59	15.41	16.29	17.23	18.25	19.38
Discus	56.18m	51.40m	46.60m	41.72m	36.80m	31.78m	26.68m
Pole Vault	5.29m	4.97m	4.64m	4.30m	3.94m	3.57m	3.18m
Javelin	77.20m	70.68m	64.10	57.46m	50.74m	43.96m	37.06m
1500 Meters	3:53.79	4:07.42	4:21.77	4:36.96	4:53.20	5:10.73	5:29.96

Here is what the approximate incremental performances are worth:

100 Meters	0.10 sec =	22 pts	or	10 pts =	0.05 sec
Long Jump	10 cm =	24 pts	or	10 pts =	4 cm
Shot Put	50 cm =	30 pts	or	10 pts =	15 cm
High Jump	3 cm =	28 pts	or	10 pts =	1 cm
400 Meters	0.50 sec =	24 pts	or	10 pts =	0.20 sec
110m Hurdles	0.10 sec =	12 pts	or	10 pts =	0.08 sec
Discus	1 meter =	20 pts	or	10 pts =	50 cm
Pole Vault	10 cm =	30 pts	or	10 pts =	3 cm
Javelin	1 meter =	15 pts	or	10 pts =	65 cm
1500 Meters	5 seconds=	34 pts	or	10 pts =	1.5 sec

Here is a very abbreviated metric conversion for the six field events:

Long Jump	Shot Put	High Jump	Discus	Pole Vault	Javelin
5.00m=18$^{1/2}$	10.00m=32-9$^{3/4}$	1.60m=5-3	25.00m=82-0	2.50m=8-2$^{1/2}$	35.00m=114-10
6.00m=19-8$^{1/4}$	11.00m=36-1$^{1/4}$	1.70m=5-7	30.00m=98-5	3.00m=9-10	40.00m=131-3
6.50m=21-4	12.00m=39-4$^{1/2}$	1.80m=5-10$^{3/4}$	35.00m=114-7	3.50m=11-5$^{3/4}$	45.00m=147-8
7.00m=22-11$^{3/4}$	13.00m=42-8	1.90m=6-2$^{3/4}$	40.00m=131-3	4.00m=13-1$^{1/2}$	50.00m=164-0
7.50m=24-7$^{1/4}$	14.00m=45-11	2.00m=6-6$^{3/4}$	45.00m=147-8	4.50m=14-9	55.00m=180-5
8.00m=26-3	15.00m=49-2$^{1/2}$	2.10m=6-10$^{3/4}$	50.00m=164-0	5.00m=16-4$^{3/4}$	60.00m=196-10
8.80m=28-10$^{1/2}$	16.00m=52-6	2.20m=7-2$^{1/2}$	55.00m=180-5	5.50m=18$^{1/2}$	65.00m=213-3

9

A FEW REMINDERS

For Athletes

- Do the best you can in each event, remembering that you are attempting to be the overall champion in 10 events.

- The score is the important thing. Winning each single event is not. At the 1995 IAAF World Championship, Dan O'Brien did not win one event outright, yet won the decathlon by more than 200 points. For the most part, decathletes compete against themselves while keeping a wary eye on the opposition.

- The decathlon offers the chance to recuperate from a mistake. Foul up in one event and there is still hope.

- Think positively, preventing failure in one event from spilling over to the next event. And, please, remain in the contest and finish, even if things are not going well.

- Be aggressive to the end. Even in the 1500 meters, be greedy and go for as many points as you can possibly run up.

- Be familiar with the rule book.

- Many of the decathlon's psychological problems (nervousness, stress, anxiety) can be resolved by good organization. Good warm ups are beneficial both physiologically and psychologically. Nothing helps like being prepared.

- The decathlon is the most social of track events and promotes the greatest sense of camaraderie among the contestants. If you offer assistance, advice, implements you'll receive the same in return.

- The decathlon is more than a physical test. It is a test of character and attitude. Your attitude should, must always be positive.

- Take pride in the records you set but remember that the only records you *own* are personal ones. You don't own world, national, or meet records. You are just holding them until someone else comes along and breaks them. Sooner or later, someone will. Records do not last forever.

- If you do not intend to finish, you should not start.

- Honor your competitors with your best effort. Expect nothing less than their best. Bruce Jenner was fond of saying, "I love my competitors because they bring out the best in me."

- Thank officials after the competition.

For Coaches

- Athletes seldom make a long-term commitment to the decathlon at an early age. Rather, their interest is likely to evolve, especially after some early successes. The coach's responsibility is to nurture that interest.

- Do not expect athletes to set personal records in every event in every meet. Potential decathletes may be soured by their coaches expecting too much too soon.

- Summing a decathlete's personal records is no way to project a final score or a qualifying score. Exaggerating performances and scores on entry blanks takes a spot away from someone more deserving.

- Nothing hurts a meet (and the decathlete) as much as entering an athlete who obviously is not prepared for that level of competition. Observe entry and qualification standards.

- Be positive but realistic about how long it takes to improve and reach national and world-class levels. It has taken six years, on average, for the present crop of American 8000-plus decathletes to reach that level. Score increases are likely to accumulate significantly in early years, then taper off. No athlete can add 300 points annually to his PR. Physiology and the scoring tables do not work that way.

- Have patience. Be flexible.

- Decathlon coaches may find coaching a group very practical. When group allegiance is established, athletes can learn from and encourage one another.

- Collegiate coaches need to spell out team duties for decathletes *before* the season begins. This includes the number of decathlons to be contested, responsibilities in dual meets and more. Under no circumstances ask a decathlete to handle relay duty immediately after a decathlon.

- Do not recruit a young athlete as a decathlete unless you are willing to train him as a decathlete first. Track and field athletes who are treated as "secondary" decathletes are unsuccessful.

- Don't be afraid to use assistant coaches. If you do, then attend as many sessions as possible conducted by the assistant coach. Make sure that coaches communicate and that workouts fit the overall scheme of a decathlete's training regime.

- Know the rules.

For Parents & Spouses

- Attend as many competitions as possible. From the athlete's standpoint, it is useful to show support for his efforts. But remember, there is a difference between parental support and parental pressure. Sometimes young athletes feel pressure *because* their parents are in attendance. It's important for the athlete to know that parents will be supportive no matter what the final score or place.

- Always encourage your child to finish the entire decathlon. The one exception is if he is injured.

- Don't brag about your child's accomplishments. Remember, the world-recordholder's family might be seated directly behind you.

For Spectators

Photo courtesy of Iris Hensel

Spectators should get as close to the action as possible. Sitting on the infield during field events puts you in the middle of the action.

Keep score. It will give you something to do. Both the IAAF Scoring Tables and *Track and Field News' Big Red Book* have small, introductory sections on how to keep score. Bring paper and pencils.

Have patience. The rules suggest (and athletes maintain) that there should be at least 30 minutes rest between events. Consequently, spectators view a lot of resting.

If you intend to survive, here are a few suggestions concerning what to bring or do between events:

- Bring your breakfast.
- Bring a cushion for the creeping numbness in the hindquarters.
- Bring a dozen pencils and a scorecard.
- Bring your lunch.
- Learn the metric system.
- Bring a book or magazine.
- Listen to the announcer.
- Bring a radio or laptop computer (or both).
- Bring rain gear.
- Bring your dinner
- Bring a quarter for a phone call explaining why you'll be late getting home.
- Be encouraging and noncritical. Get involved. Intend to survive. It takes stamina to be a decathlon spectator.

10

FURTHER
READING

The decathlete may be interested in additional books
or articles on decathlon-related topics. The author
suggests the following titles:

Ancient Olympics

Young, D. (1984) *The Olympic Myth of Greek Amateur
Athletics*. Chicago: Ares Publishers.

Modern Olympic Games

The Associated Press and Grollier. (1979) *Pursuit of
Excellence, The Olympic Story*. New York: Franklin
Watts.

Kamper, E. & Mallon, B. (1992) *The Golden Book of the
Olympic Games*. Milan: Vallardi & Associates.

Mallon, B. & Buchanan, I. (1984, et al) *Quest for Gold:
The Encyclopedia of American Olympians*. New York:
Leisure Press.

Wallechinsky, D. (1991) *The Complete Book of the
Olympics*. Boston: Little Brown.

Modern Track & Field History

Quercetani, R. (1990) *Athletics: A History of Modern Track and Field Athletics, 1860-1990.* Milan: Lallardi & Associates.

Decathlon History

Jenner, B., & Finch, P. (1977) *Decathlon Challenge: Bruce Jenner's Story.* Englewood Cliffs, NJ: Prentice Hall

Johnson, D. with Becker, V. (1995) *Aim High: An Olympic Decathlete's Inspiring Story.* Grand Rapids, MI: Zondervan Publishing.

Newcombe, J. (1975) *The Best of the Athletic Boys.* Garden City, NY.: Doubleday.

Wheeler, R.W. (1975*) Jim Thorpe, World's Greatest Athlete.* Norman OK, University of Oklahoma Press.

Rozin, S. (1983) *Daley Thompson: The Subject is Winning.* London: Stanley Paul & Company, Ltd.

Zarnowski, Frank (1989) *Decathlon: A Colorful History of Track's Most Challenging Event.* Champaign, IL: Leisure Press.

Decathlon Training

Doherty, K. (1985) *Track and Field OMNIBOOK*, 4th ed., Mountain View, CA: Tafnews Press. (Chapter on decathlon training)

Lease, D. (1990) *Combined Events.* 3rd ed. Birmingham: British Amateur Athletic Board (BAAB)

Nutrition, Steroids, Injuries

Roy, S. & Irvin, R. (1983) *Sports Medicine: Prevention, Evaluation, Management & Rehabilitation.* Englewood Cliffs, NJ: Prentice Hall, Inc.

Wright, J.E. & Cowart, V.S. (1990) *Anabolic Steriods: Altered States.* Carmel, IN: Benchmark Press.

Goulart, F. (1985) *The Official Eating to Win Cookbook: Super Foods for Super Athletic Performance.* New York: Stein & Day

Rules and Scoring Tables

IAAF Official Handbook, 1995/96 (1995). Monte Carlo: International Amateur Athletic Federation (IAAF).

Editors of Track & Field News, (1995) *Big Red Book.* Mountain View, CA.: Tafnews Press.

1996 Competition Rules for Athletics (1996). Indianapolis: USA Track & Field.

"Scoring Tables for Men's and Women's Combined Events Competitions." (1995) Monte Carlo: International Amateur Athletic Federation.

Simmons, M., Ed. (1995) *NCAA Track & Field/Cross Country Men's and Women's Rules.* Mission, KS: The National Collegiate Athletic Association.

Records

van Kuijen, H. (ed) (1996). "1995 Annual Report, Combined Events"(annual). de Bergen 66, 5706 RZ Helmond, Netherlands.

Zarnowski, F., et. al. (1996) "Decathlon/Heptathlon Handbook" (annual). Indianapolis: USA Track and Field.

Newsletters

"DECA Newsletter," c/o Frank Zarnowski, DECA, The Decathlon Association, Mount St. Mary's College, Emmitsburg, Maryland 21727 USA (eight issues per year).

▶11

THE RECORD PAGE

Outdoor

World & American

8891   Dan O'Brien/USA   Talence, FRA   1992
(10.43 808 1669 207 48.51 13.98 4856 500 6258 4:42.10)

World Junior

8397   Thorsten Voss/GDR   Erfut, GDR   1982
(10.76 766 1441 200 48.37 14.37 4176 480 6290 4:34.04)

American Junior

7658   Keith Robinson/BYU   Houston, TX   1983
(11.02 674 1248 200 49.65 15.04 4422 430 5440 4:24.38)

High School

7359   Craig Brigham/S Eugene HS
                    Eugene, OR   1972
(10.9 673 1418 193 52.3 15.5 4416 443 6024 4:53.0)

Collegiate

8322   Mike Ramos/U of Wash. Los Angeles   1986
(10.77 739 1487 216 50.16 14.99 4906 480 6352 4:48.06)

Olympic Games

8847   Daley Thompson/GBR   Los Angeles, 1984
(10.44 801 1572 203 46.97 14.33 4656 500 6524 4:35.00)

One Hour Decathlon

7897   Robert Zmelik/Czech Repub
                          Ostrava,Czech Repub   1992
(10.89 764 1452 208 55.53 14.25 4192 480 6034 4:55.16)

Pentathlon

4282   Bill Toomey/USA   London, GBR   1969
(758 6618 21.3 4453 4:20.3)

Indoor

Heptathlon

6476   Dan O'Brien/USA   Toronto, CAN   1993
(6.67 784 1602 213 7.85 520 2:57.96)

Pentathlon

4497   Dan O'Brien/USA   Moscow, ID 1992
(track > 200m) (7.88 735 1469 215 2:40.12)

Pentathlon

4478   Steve Fritz/USA   Manhattan, KS   1995
(track = 200m) (7.87 748 1613 206 2:45.32)

ᵮ12

A DECATHLETE'S ADDRESS BOOK

AAAD (American Athletic Association of the Deaf)

Executive Director
3607 Washington Blvd. #4
Ogden, UT 84403-1737
phone: 801-393-7916
fax: 801-393-2263

AAU Junior Olympics

c/o Don Kavades
National Track and Field Director
P.O. Box 1433
283 N. South St.
Porterville, CA 93250
phone: 209-784-5485

ABC Radio's Vic Holchak

Toll Free Track & Field
Radio Reports
phone: 1-800-96-TRACK

American Track & Field

Larry Eder, Publisher
Shooting Star Media, Inc.
16 E. Portola Avenue
Los Altos, CA 94022
phone: 415-949-2072

Athletics Canada

(Canadian Track and Field Federation)
1600 James Naismith Drive
Gloucester, Ontario K18 5N4
Canada
phone: 613-748-5678

Atlanta Committe for the Olympic Games (ACOG)

250 Williams St, Suite 6000
Atlanta, GA 30303
phone: 404-224-1996
(Games dates: July 20-August 4, 1996)

Dan O'Brien Youth Foundation

P.O. Box 357
Klamath Falls, OR 97601
phone: 503-884-2284

For more information about the National High School Invitational Decathlon:

Mike Keller, Track Coach
University of Idaho
Kibbie Center
Moscow, ID 83843
phone: 208-885-0210

Deaf Athletics

Don Boyer
c/o Middletown High School
Middletown, MD 21769

Jack Mike, Track Coach
Gallaudet University
800 Florida Ave., N.E.
Washington, D.C. 20002
phone: 202-651-5603

DECA, The Decathlon Assn.

c/o Frank Zarnowski
Mount St. Mary's College
Emmitsburg, MD 21727
phone: 301-447-6122

High School Decathlons

Brigham Young Invitational (held early May)
c/o BYU PE Services, RB 112
Provo, UT 84602
801-378-3994

Glendale Invitational (held early April)
Carol Torrance
3412 W. Glenrose
Phoenix, AZ 85017
602-336-2934

Great SouthWest Decathlon (held late May)
Ed Hedges, c/o Central High School
4525 N. Central
Phoenix, AZ 85012
602-274-8100

New England High School (held early July)
John Buckley
14 Stagecoach Rd.
Hingham, MA 02043
617-749-1308

Ultimate Athlete Spring (held late April)
Westerville, OH

Human Kinetics Publishers
(Publishers of The Decathlon)
Box # 5076
Champaign, IL 61825
phone: 1-800-747-4457

IAAF (International Amateur Athletic Federation)
17 Rue Princesse Florentine
Monte Carlo, MC 98000
Monaco
phone: 33-9-330-7070

IOC (International Olympic Committee)

Chateau de Vidy
CH-1007 Lausanne
Switzerland
phone: 41-21-621-6111

National Indoor Scholastic Championship

Tracy Sundlun
c/o Metropolitan Assoc. of USATF
57 Reade St.
New York, NY 10007-1821
phone: 212-227-0071

National Masters News

Subscription Dept.
P.O. Box 16597
North Hollywood, CA 91615
phone: 818-577-7233

NAIA (National Association of Intercollegiate Athletics)

6120 S. Yale Ave., Suite 1450
Tulsa, OK 74136
phone: 918-494-8828

National Track and Field Hall of Fame Historical Research Library

c/o Rare Books Collections Librarian
Irwin Library
Butler University
4600 Sunset Ave.
Indianapolis,. IN 46208
phone: 317-283-9265

NCAA (National Collegiate Athletic Association)

6201 College Blvd.
Overland Park, KS 66211
phone: 913-339-1906

NFSHSAA (National Federation of State High School Athletic Associations)

P.O. Box 206206
Kansas City, MO 64195
phone: 816-464-5400

NJCAA (National Junior College Athletic Association)

P.O. Box 7305
Colorado Springs, CO 80933
phone: 719-590-9788

Special Olympics
Director of Track and Field
Special Olympics International
1350 New York Ave., N.W.
Suite 500
Washington, D.C. 20005
phone: 202-628-3630
fax: 202-737-1937

T&FN (Track & Field News)
2570 El Camino Real, (Suite 606)
Mountain View, CA 94040
phone: 415-948-8188

USABA (United States Assoc. of Blind Athletes)
Dr. Roger Neppi, Executive Director
United States Assoc. of Blind Athletes
33 North Institute St.
Brown Hall, Suite 015
Colorado Springs, CO 80903
phone: 719-630-0422
fax: 719-630-0616

(USATF) USA Track & Field
Box # 120
One RCA Dome, Suite 140
Indianapolis, IN 46225
phone: 317-261-0500

For information about state associations:
W. Curtis Stitt   home: 614-237-6513
2605 Wellesley Road
Columbus, OH 43209

For information about calendar events:
Press Information Office   office:317-261-0500
USA Track and Field   fax: 317-261-0481
One Hoosier Dome, Suite 140
Indianapolis, IN 46225

For information about masters and veterans track programs:
Barbara Kousky   home: 503-687-8787
5319 Donald Street   office: 503-687-1989
Eugene, OR 97405-4820   fax: 503-687-1016

USATF Youth Athletics:
Kim L. Haines   home: 406-677-2427
PO Box 416   office: 406-677-2224
Seeley Lake, MT 59868   fax: 406-677-2949

USATF, Chair of Decathlon Olympic Development Committee
Fred Samara
Track Coach
Princeton University
c/o Jadwyn Gym
Princeton, N.J. 08544
phone: 609-258-5007

USOC (United States Olympic Committee)
One Olympic Plaza
Colorado Springs, CO 80909
phone: 719-632-5551

VISA, USA Decathlon Team
Coach Harry Marra
VISA USA, Inc.
P.O. Box # 8999
San Francisco, CA 94128

Veteran/Masters Decathlon
Rex Harvey   home: 216-446-0559
160 Chatham Way
Mayfield Heights, OH 44124

See also USATF and WAVA

WAVA (World Association of Veteran Athletes)
Barbara Kousky   home: 503-687-8787
5319 Donald St.   office: 503-687-1989
Eugene, OR 97405   fax: 503-687-1016

GLOSSARY

Like all sports, track and field has a language of its own. Knowing the language, using the correct terms and designating the proper sports organizations will facilitate understanding for the decathlete, coach, official, parent and spectator.

AAU—The Amateur Athletic Union is a national organization that offers, among other sports, a Junior Olympic track and field program. It was formerly the national track federation. Its duties were turned over to The Athletic Congress (TAC) in 1979. TAC changed its name to USA Track and Field in 1993.

Aerobic—Sustained exercise, like jogging or calisthenics, designed to stimulate and strengthen the heart without causing a loss of oxygen to the muscles. Literally, "with oxygen."

Anaerobic—Exercise, like sprinting, designed to strengthen the heart while muscles loose oxygen. Literally, "in the absence of oxygen."

Anabolic Steroids—Hormones, especially testosterone, that promote growth of muscle tissue. Anabolic steroids have been banned by all track and field organizations which periodically test athletes for its presence. Positive tests may result in bans.

Automatic Timing—Timing accomplished by an electronic device that discriminates 1/100th of a second. All major track meets now use automatic timing. It is required for world-record status.

Ballistic—Sudden, very rapid, powerful movements.

Blocks—Starting blocks, placed behind the starting line, are used by sprinters/hurdlers in races of 400 meters and less as an aid in starting.

Dan O'Brien Youth Foundation—Founded in 1992 and named after the current decathlon world-recordholder, this foundation raises scholarship funds for needy youths, promotes citizenship and offers a national high school decathlon championship.

DECA—The Decathlon Association is a non-profit organization whose purpose is to promote the decathlon, publish and disseminate decathlon training information, meet schedules, results and record information. Publishes the "DECA Newsletter" eight times annually.

DecaStar—An annual international elite decathlon invitational meet held in Talence, France.

Discus—A circular disk, usually made of wood with a metal rim, that is thrown. The seventh event of the decathlon.

Endurance Running—Long-distance running. Usually, distances include the marathon (26.2 miles) and longer. For decathletes, any training for the 1500 meters.

Fartlek—A Swedish term meaning "speed play." It is a running workout, used frequently by distance runners, wherein the speed is altered frequently. Calisthenics are interspersed with the run.

Götzis—A small town in the Austrian Alps which annually conducts a popular international decathlon.

Heats—Sections of a running event. For races run in lanes, no fewer than three should start in any heat, and no more than the number of lanes.

Heptathlon—A seven-event track and field competition. For men, it is held indoors and consists of the 60-meter hurdles, long jump, shot put and high jump on the first day and the 60-meter hurdles, pole vault and 1000-meter run on the second day. The IAAF recognizes and official world record for this event. For women, the heptathlon is the counterpart of the decathlon. It is held outdoors and consists of the 100-meter hurdles, high jump, long jump and 200 meters on the first day. On the second day the events are the long jump, javelin and 800 meters.

High Jump—The decathlon's fourth event wherein the competitor, using a running start and leaping off one foot, jumps for height over a crossbar.

Hurdles—A race over a series of ten 42-inch barriers (39 inches for high school athletes) over 110 meters. The decathlon's sixth event.

IAAF—The International Amateur Athletic Federation is the governing body for track and field worldwide. The IAAF sets rules, provides scoring tables and offers, at two-year intervals, a world track and field championship. Home offices recently moved from London to Monte Carlo.

IC4A—The Intercollegiate Amateur Athletic Association of America is the oldest collegiate track and field conference. Its current members are mostly East Coast universities.

Imperial System—An English system of measurement used primarily in the United States. The basic units of measurement are the inch, foot, yard and mile. The decathlon does not use Imperial distances.

Interval Training—A training routine in which the athlete runs a series a specified distances for time separated by designated rest periods or "intervals." Depending upon the speed of the runs, the workout can become anaerobic.

IOC—The International Olympic Committee is responsible for the Olympic Games.

Javelin—A light spear, usually made of metal, which is thrown for distance, it is approximately 8-1/2 feet in length with a cord handle and weighs 800 grams (1.76 pounds). The decathlon's next-to-last (ninth) event.

Junior—A young athlete who does not turn age 20 in the current year. There are national and world "junior" championships.

Long Jump—A leap for distance into a sand landing pit that uses a running start. Formerly called the "broad jump" in the United States. The decathlon's second event.

Manual Timing—Timing accomplished by hand (stop watch) to within 1/10th of a second. Digital watches that record times to within 1/100th of a second are a form of manual timing and results must be rounded up (for example, 10.78 becomes 10.8).

Master—A master competitor must be at least 40 years old. There is a sub-master level beginning at age 35.

Metric System—An international system of measurement whose main units of length for track and field purposes are the meter (approximately 39 inches) and centimeter (approximately 0.4 inch). All decathlon track events are listed in meters (for example, 100 meters, 400 meters, and all field events are measured in meters and centimeters.

NAIA—The National Association of Intercollegiate Athletics is a national organization of small colleges and universities. The first national collegiate organization (1969) to offer a decathlon championship.

NCAA—The National Collegiate Athletic Association is the governing body for most of America's colleges and universities. The NCAA provides rules for its members and offers a decathlon championship.

Olympic Games—A quadrennial celebration wherein approximately 200 nations participate. The Olympic decathlon champion is often referred to as the "World's Greatest Athlete."

Pentathlon—A five-event contest. Outdoors, the traditional pentathlon consists of the long jump, javelin, 200 meters, discus and 1500 meters. Indoors, the events usually include 60-meter or 55-meter hurdles, long jump, shot put, high jump and 1000 meters. The historical forerunner of the decathlon.

Pole Vault—The decathlon's eighth event, wherein the athlete attempts to clear a crossbar with the use of a long (12–17 feet) vaulting pole. A foam rubber landing pit is necessary beyond the crossbar.

Power Training—Lifting weights, for example, barbells, in a prescribed manner for the purpose of enhancing strength. Useful mostly for the decathlon throwing events.

Shot Put—The third decathlon event in which a 16-pound metal ball is pushed or put for distance. High school students use a 12-pound put.

Sprints—A race at full speed for a short distance. Examples are the 100-meter and 400-meter races. The 100-meter sprint is the decathlon's initial event. Starting blocks are used and the athlete responds to the commands and pistol of a starter.

Talence—A suburb of Bordeaux, France, that annually sponsors a major international decathlon called DecaStar.

TAC—The Athletic Congress was the successor to the AAU and preceded USATF as the governing body for all sanctioned track and field in the United States.

USATF—United States of America Track and Field is America's national governing body for the sport. As with other track governing bodies, USATF offers rules, maintains records and conducts and sanctions national championships for both junior and senior athletes and regional competitions.

USOC—The United States Olympic Committee organizes the U.S. Olympic teams every 4 years. The USOC also conducts national training centers in Colorado Springs and Chula Vista, California.

Veteran—A veteran competitor is at least 40 years old. The term *veteran* is often used interchangeably with *master*. The difference is that *master* is used primarily in the United States while *veteran* is used primarily in international contexts.

VISA, USA, Inc.—An American credit card company which sponsors, provides financial support and conducts clinics for a national decathlon team and promotes grass roots, regional and national decathlon meets.

WAVA—The World Association of Veteran Athletes sponsors a world championship for masters-age competitors, maintains veteran records and sets rules for veteran track and field.

Wind—For decathlon-record purposes, the aiding wind (tailwinds) in the 100 meters, long jump and 110-meter hurdles cannot exceed 4 mps (meters per second). The rule is 2 mps for open track and field events.

World Record—The highest total decathlon score officially approved by the IAAF. At the end of 1995, Dan O'Brien's 8891 points were the world record. Since 1911, the world record has been broken 56 times.

Don't Miss...

A New Book About Decathlon History...

OLYMPIC GLORY DENIED

by Frank Zarnowski

Biographical profiles of 11 of the world's greatest athletes, all of whom, for reasons beyond their control, never reached the Olympic starting line. This new, lively work features portraits of great track athletes like Fait Elkins, Charley Hoff and Heino Lipp. For the most part they are forgotten ghosts of yesteryear, never able to take claim of the mantle, Olympic decathlon champion. Only one name is recognizable to most readers, that of current world record holder Dan O'Brien. In 1992 O'Brien failed to make the US Olympic team. But unlike his ten predecessors, O'Brien will have another opportunity.

$18.95
Published by:
Griffin Publishing
544 W. Colorado Street
Glendale, CA 91204

phone: 1-818-244-2128

ISBN 1-882180-70-4

Available at your favorite book store, from the publisher, or the author:

Frank Zarnowski, Ph.D.
Mt. St. Mary's College,
Emmitsburg, MD 21727
USA.